ISBN 978-0-265-92077-0
PIBN 10909999

Vaughan's Seeds 1913

Chicago. New York.

Wholesale Prices for the Trade

THIS LIST CANCELS ALL PREVIOUS OFFERS

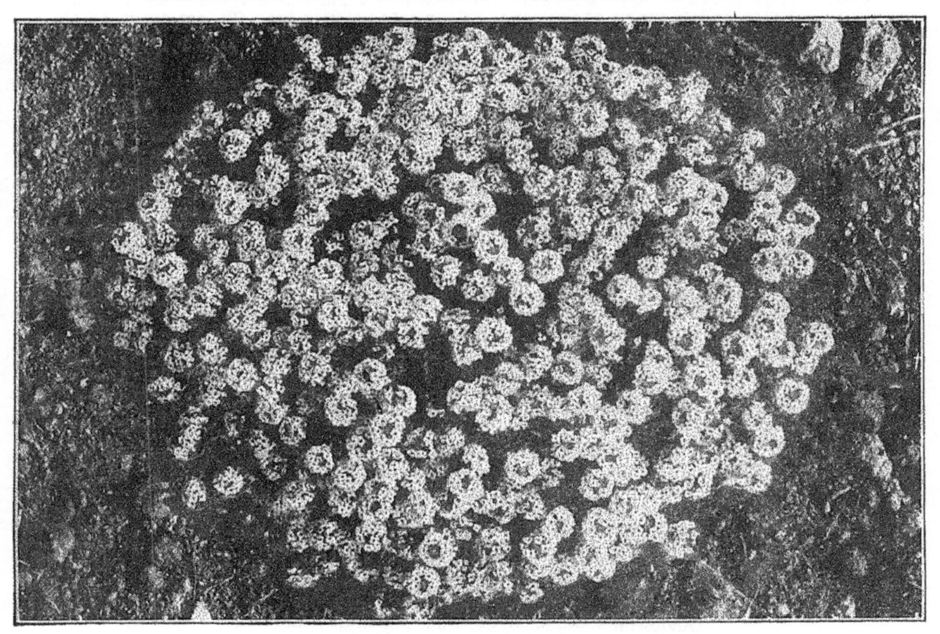

ALYSSUM VAUGHAN'S LITTLE GEM—Selected Stock

Vegetable and Flower Seeds, Bulbs and Plants

POULTRY SUPPLIES, TOOLS, ETC.

VAUGHAN'S SEED STORE

CHICAGO 31-33 W. Randolph St. NEW YORK 25 Barclay St.

Greenhouses, Nurseries and Trial Grounds, Western Springs, Ill.

BUSINESS CONDITIONS.

Trade Discount from General Catalogue—Orders taken from our General Descriptive Catalogue will be charged at the following rate of discount from our retail prices.

Seeds in packets: 33⅓ per cent. discount on orders under $2.00, 50 per cent. discount (except novelties, on which we allow 30 per cent.) on orders exceeding $2.00.

(When ordering in lots of 500 packets or over, 60 per cent.)

Seeds by the ounce, 33⅓ per cent. discount.
Seeds by the quart or pint, 30 per cent. discount.
Plants at 20 per cent. off prices for single plants.
10 per cent. on "Special Offers" and "Collections."

These discounts apply only when order amounts to not less than $1.00

Seeds by Mail.—*On all stock mailed postage will be charged to purchaser, including registry fee (or prepaid express), if package exceeds $2.00 in value. We do not assume risk of loss by mail unless registered or insured.*

Quantity Prices on Flower Seeds.—We furnish not less than ¼ pounds at the pound rate, and ¼ ounces at the ounce rate, where not less than 60c. per ounce, except where a special price is quoted. We do not sell less than one ounce of any sort listed at 15c. per ounce or less.

TERMS.—Sixty days net cash to Seed Houses of approved credit, except on cash items named below, or on special quotations. Seed houses buying their general supply from us will be given June 1st terms. Bills to houses not regularly in the catalogue seed trade are due the first of every month following date of purchase. Grass, Farm, Bird and Clover Seeds, Onion Sets, Potatoes, Fertilizers, Bone Mills, Raphia, Reeds, Insecticides, Mushroom Spawn and Flower Pots, are always net cash.

CASH DISCOUNT.—We allow a discount of 1 per cent. per month for cash with order, and also on bills paid within 10 days of date of invoice, (excepting cash items mentioned before).

The prices in this catalogue are subject to advance, without notice and cancel all former quotations.

Routing Shipments.—Railroad or Express routes given by buyers, which should be on each order, will be strictly followed by us where possible. In all cases where the route is left to our judgment we will select the best we know, but entirely at the risk of the buyer, we assuming no responsibility for delays in transportation.

NOT WARRANTED.—We do not warrant in any way, express, or implied, the contents, or the description, quality, productiveness, or any other matter of any seeds, bulbs or plants, sold by us, and we will not be in any way responsible for the crop. If the purchaser does not accept these goods on the above terms, no sale is made thereof, and he must return them at once, and money will be refunded. Subject to above conditions we make this sale, at the moderate prices at which we sell our goods. Vaughan's Seed Store (Incorporated)

Electrotypes of most of our illustrations in retail catalogue can be furnished at 15 cents per square inch.

TELEGRAPHIC WORDS FOR QUANTITIES.

AMOUNT.	OZ.	LB.	BUSHEL.
⅛	Quandem	Quanode	Quaphis
¼	Quananas	Quanoint	Quaphony
½	Quanarch	Quanoka	Quaphote
¾	Quanback	Quanold	Quapiary
1	Quanbrum	Quanolis	Quapices
2	Quanbury	Quanomia	Quapist
3	Quanceps	Quanomy	Quapilz
4	Quancile	Quanon	Quapium
5	Quancome	Quanopsy.	Quaplin
10	Quanders	Quanrush	Quapode
15	Quanear	Quanta	Quapolus
20	Quanewal	Quantic.	Quapozem
25	Quangina	Quaocus	Quappeal
30	Quangor	Quaoler	Quappian
40	Quanimus.	Quaostos.	Quaplate
50	Quannark.	Quapepsy.	Quarado
100	Quashfly	Quatrium	Quaxil

A. B. C. Code used. 4th and 5th Edition.

J. C. VAUGHAN, PRES.
L. H. VAUGHAN, VICE-PRES.
C. CROPP, SEC'Y. & TREAS.

Vaughan's Seed Store.

ESTABLISHED 1876.
INCORPORATED 1901.

When possible and so requested, we will so far as our stock permits hold these prices f. o. b. New York City, but we do not guarantee to do so in any case since the bulk of our stock is carried in Chicago.

Vaughan's Seed Store

NEW YORK:
25 BARCLAY STREET

CHICAGO:
31-33 W. RANDOLPH STREET

WEST SIDE BRANCH:
803 WEST RANDOLPH STREET.

Greenhouses and Trial Grounds: Western Springs, Ill.

Trade List of Seeds.

Our stocks are the very best and will satisfy the most critical retail and market gardener's trade. We do not handle two grades, one for our own retail business and another cheaper line for the jobbing trade.

We own our seeds at right prices. In the present season of extreme short crops there is bound to be considerable variation in the prices of the different jobbers—especially since the cheaper strains of certain vegetables are in fair supply whereas the better class are almost out of the market. If certain items seem out of line, write us, stating quantity desired and we will meet reliable prices.

ARTICHOKE.	Tel. cipher.	Lb.	100 lbs.
Green Globe	Abaddon	$1.75	
Tubers (Jerusalem), bu, $1.25; bbl. of 2¾ bu., $3.00; if shipped from New York, bu., $1.50; bbl., $3.75	Abatis		

ASPARAGUS SEED.		Lb.	100 lbs.
Bonvallet's Giant, new	Asval	.75	
Early Giant Argenteuil	Astor	.40	
Palmetto	Assurge	.25	$22.00
Conover's Colossal	Aspen	.25	22.00
Barr's Mammoth	Ascetic	.25	22.00
Columbian Mammoth White	Askag	.35	30.00

ASPARAGUS PLANTS.	
Conover's Colossal, 1-year-old roots, per 100, 40c; per 1,000, $3.25;	Attend
2-year-old roots, per 100, 50c; per 1,000, $4.00	Atfile
Barr's Mammoth, 1-year-old roots, per 100, 40c; 1,000, $3.25	Attic
2-year-old roots, per 100, 50c; per 1,000, $4.00	Atter
Columbian Mammoth White, 1-year-old, per 100, 40c; per 1,000, $3.25	Auer
2-year-old, per 100, 50c; per 1,000, $4.00	Aueric
Bonvallet's Giant, 1-year-old, per 100, 65c; per 1,000, $5.00	Avict
2-year-old roots, per 100, 85c; per 1,000, $7.00	Avicting
Palmetto, 1-year-old roots, per 100, 40c; per 1,000, $3.25	Avern
2-year-old, per 100, 50c; per 1,000, $4.00	Avernel

STRINGLESS GREEN-POD BEANS.

BUSH BEANS.

Market Fluctuates, Write or Wire Us.

We ourselves grow the majority of our beans and we know no better qualities can be purchased anywhere.

	Tel. cipher.	Bu.	10 Bush. Per Bu.
GREEN BEANS.			
Red Valentine, Improved Earliest	Blacklash	$4.25	$4.00
Refugee, or 1,000 to 1	Barrack	4.50	4.25
Extra Early Refugee	Baleful	4.75	4.50
Stringless Green Pod	Baste	5.25	5.00
Giant Stringless Green Pod	Bash	4.75	4.50
Black Valentine	Basis	4.25	4.00
Bountiful	Barratary	4.25	4.00
Broad Windsor	Bacchanal	6.00	5.75
Dwarf Horticultural	Bankhouse	4.75	4.50
Early Mohawk	Badness	4.00	3.75
Early Round Pod Six Weeks	Baker	4.00	3.75
Full Measure	Bastile	4.75	4.50
Improved Tree	Banking	3.25	3.00
Long Yellow Six Weeks	Bashful	4.00	3.75
Longfellow	Barr	4.50	4.25
Red Kidney	Battery	4.00	3.75
White Kidney	Battes	4.00	3.75
White Marrow	Batting	4.00	3.75
Triumph of the Frames, for forcing	Bassoon	pk., $4.50	
WAX BEANS.			
Currie's Rust Proof Golden Wax	Believe	4.50	4.25
Round Pod Kidney Wax (Brittle Wax)	Bibuling	5.75	5.50
Improved Dwarf Golden Wax	Besee	5.25	5.00
Davis Wax, hardiest and most productive	Bybox	5.00	4.75
Wardwell's Early Kidney Wax, one of the most profitable	Bicorn	5.25	5.00
Challenge Black Dwarf Wax	Begrune	5.00	4.75
Flageolet Violet	Benumb	5.25	5.00
Golden Eye Wax, Rust Proof	Beryme	5.00	4.75
Horticultural Wax	Bezel	4.50	4.25
Mammoth Yosemite Wax	Billett	7.00	
Monster Stringless	Besiege	7.50	
Pencil Pod Wax	Bibular	5.25	5.00
Prolific German Black Wax	Betroth	5.00	4.75

WAX BEANS—Continued.		Bu.	10 Bush. Per Bu.
Refugee Wax, Keeneys Stringless	Bewitch	$5.25	$5.00
Valentine Wax	Bybix	5.00	4.75
Hodson Wax, new	Byron	4.75	4.50
BUSH LIMAS.			
New Wonder Bush Lima	Bilous	6.00	5.75
Henderson's Bush Lima	Binmack	5.75	5.50
Burpee's Bush Lima	Billow	6.00	5.75
Dreer's Bush Lima	Bilton	6.75	6.50
Fordhook Bush	Brad	Sold out	
Burpee's Improved	Braddock	8.50	
BEANS, POLE.			
Early Golden Cluster Wax	Bluster	7.00	6.75
Lazy Wife	Bogale	5.25	5.00
Kentucky Wonder, or Old Homestead	Bodkin	4.75	4.50
Dutch Case Knife	Bootlag	4.75	4.50
Horticultural Cranberry	Boaster	5.25	5.00
White Creaseback	Blemish	5.00	4.75
Scarlet **Runner**	Bonton	6.75	6.50
Large Lima	Botarge	5.00	4.75
Dreer's Improved Lima	Boscage	5.50	5.25
"**King** of the **Garden" Lima**	Botanize	5.50	5.25
Ford's Mammoth Lima	Bosheit	5.50	5.25
Extra Early Jersey Lima	Bosom	5.25	5.00
Siebert's Early Lima	Bottom	5.25	5.00
Burger's Stringless	Boggy	6.00	5.75
Early Leviathan	Booth	5.75	5.50
Ideal Pole Lima	Boat	6.00	5.75
French Asparagus	Bosley	50c per lb.	
Carpinteria	Borax	7.00	

BEET.

The better grades of Beet seed this year are shorter than for many seasons. For good sized quantities write or wire us for figures.

	Tel. cipher.	Lb.	100 lbs.
Arlington	Braccate	$0.90	$80.00
Bassano, Early Flat Red	Braccio	.90	80.00
Crosby's Egyptian, American grown	Brace	1.40	
Crosby's Egyptian, Imported	Bracelet	1.25	
Early Egyptian, Improved	Bracher	.90	85.00
Crimson Globe	Brabast	1.25	115.00
Eclipse, extra select stock	Brail	.90	85.00
Early Blood Turnip	Braggard	1.00	90.00
Dewing's Early Blood **Turnip,** Select	Bract	1.00	90.00
Half Long Blood, very deep red	Brangle	1.00	
Long Smooth Dark Blood	Branch	.75	70.00
Edmand's Blood Turnip, select stock	Braja	1.00	90.00
Electric, early	Branching	1.25	
Detroit Dark Red Turnip	Brackish	1.25	
Vaughan's Chicago Market	Brent	1.35	
Swiss Chard or Summer Spinach	Bream	.35	30.00
Swiss Chard Lucullus	Breal	.45	40.00
Swiss Chard Lyon	Brete	.40	35.00
Vaughan's Fireball	Breet	1.75	

Specialties and Novelties.—It is our aim to carry a complete up-to-date line. New sorts or special strains are catalogued as soon as we become convinced of their merits. Old sorts are dropped when we consider them displaced by improved kinds. For descriptions of latest additions consult the specialty pages of our descriptive retail catalog.

	Tel. cipher.	Lb.	100 lbs.
MANGEL WURZEL.—Short Crop.			
Vaughan's Mammoth Long Red	Brigade	$0.35	$32.00
Champion Yellow Globe	Breeper	.35	30.00
Golden Tankard	Brevier	.35	30.00
Giant Yellow, Eckendorf	Brewery	.40	35.00
Giant Yellow, Intermediate	Brettice	.35	30.00
Giant Yellow, Globe	Brewing	.35	30.00
Giant Half Sugar Rose	Brewer	.40	35.00
SUGAR BEETS.—Short Crop.			
Vilmorin's Imperial White	Browning	.30	28.00
Klein's Wanzleben	Brook	.30	28.00
French Red Top	Broncho	.30	28.00
Lane's Improved White	Brora	.30	28.00
BORECOLE or KALE.			
Vaughan's Excelsior Moss Curled	Bugle	1.00	
Dwarf Green Curled Scotch	Builder	.60	55.00
Tall Green Cured Scotch	Burlesque	.65	60.00
Sea-Kale	Burgess	1.50	
Siberian	Burgher	.35	30.00
BROCCOLI. Purple Cape	Bursche	1.75	
Large White Mammoth	Bussel	1.75	
BRUSSELS SPROUTS, Paris Market	Bybond	1.00	
Improved Extra Dwarf	Bybent	1.00	
Danish Imported	Bylaw	2.25	

CABBAGE.

We call particular attention to our cabbage seed, all of which is grown in those localities and countries where the different varieties are raised to the best advantage. American varieties, Long Island grown. Seed crop again short.

	Tel. cipher.	Lb.	100 lbs.
Vaughan's Selected Jersey Wakefield	Cascane	$1.60	$150.00
Vaughan's Market Gardeners', Vandergaw, or All Seasons	Chip	1.75	160.00
Vaughan's Premium Flat Dutch	Chandler	1.40	130.00
All Head Early, or Faultless	Caravas	2.25	
Autumn King or World Beater	Carapace	1.60	150.00
Bridgeport Drumhead	Caravan	1.25	115.00
Charleston (large) Early Wakefield	Chaffer	1.50	140.00
Chinese, or Pe-Tsai	Cardel	1.00	
Danish Summer Ballhead	Carfew	1.75	160.00
Copenhagen Market (new)	Cargil	4.00	

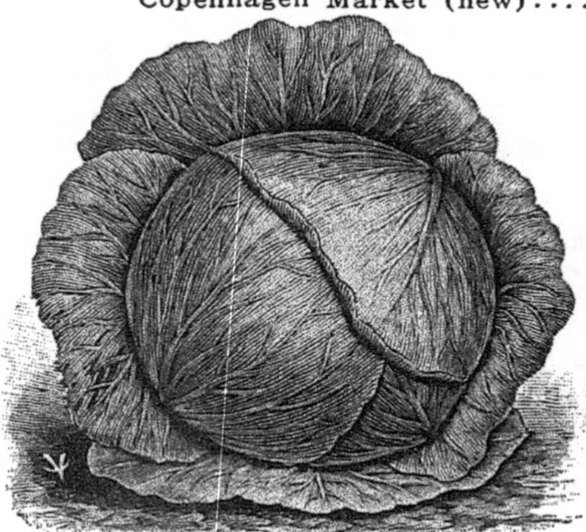

EARLY JERSEY WAKEFIELD.

VAUGHAN'S MARKET GARDENERS

CABBAGE—Continued.	Tel. cipher.	Lb.	100 lbs.
Danish Ballhead, Danish grown, tall....	Carcass	$2.00	$190.00
Danish Ballhead, Danish grown, tall.....	Carden	2.00	190.00
Dutch Winter or Hollander, true stock...	Career	2.00	190.00
Early Flat Dutch	Chawed	1.35	125.00
Early Spring	Cassop	1.60	150.00
Early Winnigstadt	Castel	1.10	100.00
Early York	Cathol	.90	85.00
Etampes, Extra Early	Carnal	1.25	115.00
Express, Extra Early (ready in 90 days)	Causer	1.25	115.00
Fottler's Imp. Brunswick Drumhead	Cedrine	1.40	135.00
Glory of **Enkhousen**	Capsize	1.65	160.00
Large Late American Drumhead, choice..	Chancel	1.25	115.00
Louisville Drumhead	Capital	1.35	125.00
Lupton	Charo	1.40	135.00
Marblehead Mammoth	Charity	1.60	150.00
New Early Flat Head	Caput	1.60	150.00
New York Early Summer, selected.....	Cassep	1.40	130.00
Stone Mason, Warren's improved	Chival	1.60	150.00
Succession	Cento	2.00	190.00
Surehead	Chintz	1.75	160.00
SAVOY CABBAGE.			
Ironhead	Cardiac	2.00	
Small Early Ulm	Cassock	1.00	
Marvin's, the very best late, true stock...	Charter	1.40	
Improved American	Cerated	1.75	
RED CABBAGE.			
Zenith, new	Cavern	2.00	
Mammoth Rock Red, large, deep red....	Chariot	2.00	
Extra Early Dark Red Erfurt..........	Cave	1.40	
Dark Red Dutch, large	Carder	1.10	
Black Diamond	Cuzer	3.25	
Red Drumhead, late red..............	Cherish	1.10	
CARDOON, Large, smooth	Concordat...	1.25	

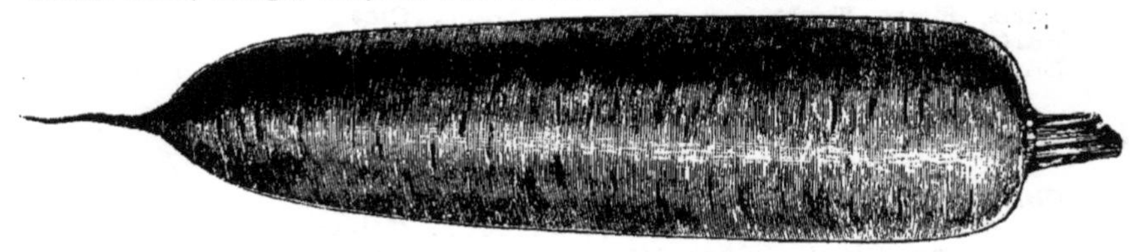

VAUGHAN'S SELECT DANVERS.

CARROT.

The carrot seed crop is again short, although it is a little better than that of last year. Our stock is from the most reliable growers and will satisfy the most critical.

Write for prices in quantity.

Inches long.		Tel. cipher.	Lb.	10 lbs.
2	Very Early Scarlet (French Horn)....	Clough	$1.40	
4	Early Short Stump Rooted.........	Clabboste	1.15	
6	**Nantes,** Half Long Scarlet, stump root	Clipper	.90	
5	**Guerande Half Long** (Oxheart).......	Cloan	.75	
6	**Chantenay,** one of the best half long..	Clabbish	.90	
8	**Danvers, (Vaughan's Selected Stock)..** only perfect roots................	Clabbax	1.00	
8	Danvers, Half Long, regular stock....	Classic	.65	
14	Improved Long Orange	Cleave	.70	
10	**White Intermediate or Mastodon**	Clincher	.65	
16	Long White Belgian, green top	Climb	.60	
16	Long Orange Belgian	Clevert	.60	

Our strains are the equal of the world's best products. Prices will be found strictly in line.

CAULIFLOWER.

	Tel. cipher.	Oz.	Lbs.
Vaughan's New Snowball	Cliver	$1.75	$24.00
Vaughan's Earliest Dwarf Erfurt	Cibospen	1.25	16.00
Dry Weather	Clip	1.75	20.00
Extra Early Dwarf Erfurt	Cicaffle	.75	10.00
Danish Snowball	Ciboskal	1.00	14.00
Algiers, large late sort Holland grown	Cibalt	.35	4.00
Autumn Giant, large and productive "	Cibank	.20	2.00
Large Early Erfurt. best for late	Cicamo	.50	6.00
Lenormand's Short Stem Mammoth	Cidade	.40	4.00
Paris, Extra Early	Cicaque	.25	3.00
Paris, Half Early, a standard early sort	Cicalve	.25	3.00
Earliest of All	Cadave	1.75	24.00

CELERY.

	Tel. cipher.	Lb.	10 lbs.
Chicago Giant Self-Blanching (best new white)	Cohan	$2.00	
Vaughan's Giant Golden Heart	Cohere	.75	$ 7.00
Golden Self-Blanching, French grown	Coiner	15.00	
Golden Self-Blanching, American grown	Coining	5.00	
Snow White, new	Compeer	1.40	12.50
Giant Pascal, a self-blanching variety	Cohort	.75	7.00
Boston Market	Coinage	.75	7.00
Crawford's Half Dwarf	Cockney	.75	7.00
Dwarf Golden Heart, the old standby	Cod	.75	7.00
Evans' Triumph	Conneaut	.75	7.00
Far Superior Many-Heart	Commey	.75	7.00
Giant White Solid	Coincide	.75	7.00
Pink Plume, excellent sort	Commander	1.25	11.00
Perfection Heartwell	Commerce	.80	7.50
Perle Le Grand	Comming	.75	7.00
Rose Ribbed Paris	Comic	2.00	
Schumacher	Compact	.80	7.50
Solid Ivory or Kalamazoo	Compile	.75	7.00
White Plume, Vaughan's selected stock	Compound	1.40	12.50
Winter Queen, hard to beat as a keeper	Compaler	.85	8.00
Soup Celery or Smallage	Coinst	.60	5.50
Old Celery Seed, for flavoring	Comet	.20	1.75
Turnip Rooted, Delicatess	Coinden	3.00	
" " Large Erfurt	Concise	2.00	
" " Large Smooth Prague	Conch	2.00	

	Tel. cipher.	Lb.
CHERVIL.		
Double curled	Concur	$0.60
CHICORY.		
Large rooted Magdeburgh	Condense	1.00
Witloof	Condescend	1.75
CHIVES, oz., 25c.	Condign	3.50
COLLARDS.		
Georgia	Condole	.40

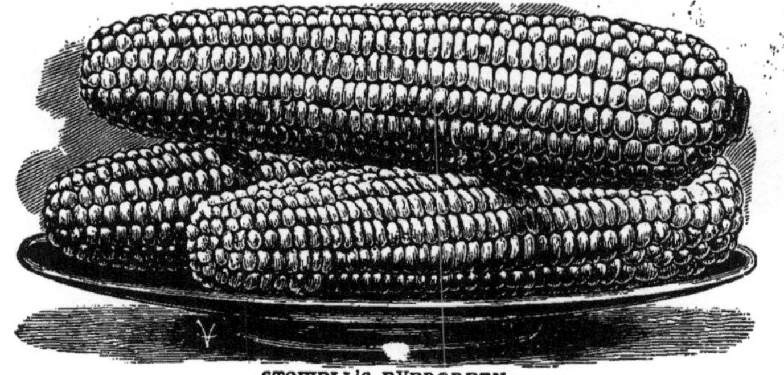

STOWELL'S EVERGREEN.

SWEET CORN (Prices unsettled. Subject to change in market.)

EARLY VARIETIES.

	Tel. cipher.	Bush.	In 10 Bu. Lots.
Malakoff, New Early corn	Confair	$4.50	
Golden Bantam, New Yellow	Confessor	3.75	3.50
Peep O'Day, very early	Confront	3.50	3.25
Premo, Extra Early	Confriar	3.25	3.00
Adams' Early, not sweet but early	Confab	2.50	2.25
Adams' Extra Early	Confabber	2.50	2.25
Crosby's Early, an excellent sort	Confluent	3.25	3.00
Champion, the earliest large sweetcorn	Confident	3.50	3.25
Cory, Mammoth White	Constituent	3.50	3.25
Early Cory, or First of All	Connate	3.25	3.00
Early Iowa	Confute	4.00	
Early Mammoth	Conjugal	3.25	3.00
Early Minnesota	Congruent	3.25	3.00
Kendal's Early Giant	Consummate	3.25	3.00
Metropolitan	Confess	3.50	3.25

MEDIUM AND LATE VARIETIES.

	Tel. cipher.	Bush.	In 10 Bu. Lots.
Black Mexican	Conference	3.25	3.00
Black Sugar, Vaughan's Eastern grown	Conferring	3.50	3.25
Country Gentleman	Conflict	3.50	3.25
Hickox Improved	Consent	3.25	3.00
Late Mammoth Sugar	Constrain	3.50	3.25
Moore's Early Concord	Consume	3.25	3.00
Old Colony, genuine Maine stock	Continent	3.25	3.00
Perry's Hybrid	Contrary	3.25	3.00
Early Evergreen	Conjunct	3.50	3.25
Evergreen Fodder	Coolly	2.00	1.75
Stowell's Evergreen, Connecticut grown	Contingent	3.25	3.00
Stowell's Evergreen, Western grown	Cooler	3.00	2.75
White Evergreen	Cooling	3.25	3.00

		lb.	10 lbs.
CORN SALAD.			
Round-Leaved, large seeded	Conductive	$0.65	

	Tel. cipher.	Lb.	10 lbs.
CRESS, CURLED GARDEN	Cuniform	$0.25	$2.25
Upland	Curracy	.45	
Water Cress, true	Currator	3.50	

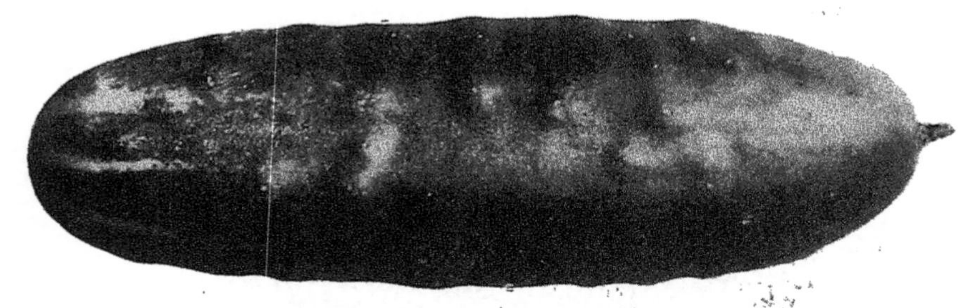

VAUGHAN'S ARLINGTON WHITE SPINE.

CUCUMBER.	Tel. cipher.	Lb.	100 lbs.
Arlington White-Spine (Vaughan's Imp.)	Creduling	$0.60	$55.00
Metcalf's White Spine (Fancy Arlington)	Cyrus	.60	55.00
Improved Chicago Pickle, true	Croft	.50	45.00
Vaughan's XXX Pickling	Cybil	.55	50.00
Jersey Pickling	Croaker	.50	45.00
Snow's Fancy Pickling	Creel	.55	50.00
Cool and Crisp	Crescent	.55	50.00
Cumberland Pickling	Croat	.55	50.00
Davis Perfect	Crost	.65	60.00
Early Cluster	Crest	.50	45.00
Early Cyclone	Culce	.55	50.00
Early Frame	Critac	.50	45.00
Emerald	Culad	.60	55.00
Evergreen, or Extra Long White Spine	Crimple	.60	55.00
Extra Early Green Prolific	Crimson	.55	50.00
Fordhook Famous	Cromlech	.60	55.00
Fordhook Pickling	Crazy	.50	45.00
Green Prolific or Boston Pickling	Croaket	.50	45.00
Improved Long Green, extra good strain	Croon	.60	55.00
Improved White Spine	Crosier	.50	45.00
Japanese Climbing	Cross	.65	60.00
Nichol's Medium Green	Crucial	.50	45.00
New Century	Croquet	.50	45.00
Rockyford (Klondyke)	Crowbar	.60	55.00
West India Gherkin	Cruch	1.00	
Carter's Model, for forcing, 1 oz., $6.00	Cubical		
Noa's Forcing, very prolific, ¼ oz., 75c.	Cully		
Prescott Wonder, ¼ oz., $1.50	Culprit		
Rollison's Telegraph, ¼ oz., $1.75	Culpably		
Vaughan's Prolific Forcing, ¼ oz., $1.00	Culvert		

	Tel. cipher.	Lb.	10 lbs.
DANDELION.—Thick Leaved or Cabbaging	Dan	3.50	
ENDIVE, Broad-leaved White	Elastic	.60	5.50
Ever-White Curled	Electric	.60	5.50
Giant Fringed	Emboss	.65	6.00
Green Curled Summer	Emblem	.60	5.50
Green Curled Winter	Embogue	.60	5.50
Moss Curled, very fine	Empress	.65	6.00
Staghorn, earliest	Elected	.65	6.00

NEW YORK IMPROVED SPINELESS.

SHORT-LEAVED EARLY ERFURT KOHLRABI.

EGG PLANT.

	Tel. cipher.	Lb.
Very Early Dwarf	Education	$1.75
Black Pekin, very early	Eager	2.25
New York Improved Spineless, best. New Jersey gardeners' selection	Edda	2.50
Black Beauty, new	Educate	3.00

GARLIC.—Sound dry bulbs. Write for prices. . Gabel
HORSE RADISH.—Horse Radish Sets, 100, 60c; 500, $2.75; 1,000, $5.
New Bohemian, per 100, $1.00; per 1,000, $8.00.

HERBS.

	Tel. ciph.	oz.	lb.
Anise	Habitat	$.05	$.50
Balm	Hackel	.12	1.50
Bene	Halcyon	.05	.50
Borage	Halser	.05	.50
Coriander	Handy	.05	.40
Caraway	Halter	.05	.20
Catnip	Halyard	.25	3.00
Chamomile	Humel	.35	3.00
Dill, 10 lbs., $3.00	Harbin	.05	.40
Fennel, Florence	Hardih	.10	.60
Fennel	Hardness	.05	.40
Henbane	Hatred	.10	
Hop	Hanter	.50	
Horehound	Haven	.10	1.25
Hyssop	Havoc	.10	1.20
Lavender Spica	Hawser	.10	.75
Lavender	Hazard	$.20	$2.25
Pennyroyal	Heads	.40	
Pimpinella	Hegira	.10	.75
Rosemary	Helical	.15	1.50
Rue	Heir	.15	1.50
Saffron	Helix	.05	.80
Sage	Helm	.10	.75
Sage.—Holt's Mam. Hardy Plants, per 100, $3.00.			
Summer Savory	Helter	.10	.75
Sweet Basil	Heptag	.10	.70
Sweet Marjoram	Heraldic	.10	.80
Thyme	Herwyn	.25	3.00
Tagetes Lucida	Heifer	.30	
Wormwood	Hiat	.10	1.20

Peppermint, per 100 seeds, 15c.; per 1000 seeds, $1.20. . Help

KOHLRABI.

	Tel. cipher	Lb.	100 lbs.
Short-leaved Early Erfurt, best strain	Knitter	$1.65	
King of the Earlies	Knit	1.75	
Early White Vienna	Kolpie	$1.00	$90.00
Early Purple Vienna	Keblap	1.10	100.00

	Tel. cipher	Lb.
LEEK. Broad Scotch	Lacerate	$1.40
Large Musselburg, of enormous size	Lactic	1.50
Rouen, Large Winter	Lama	1.50
Long Mezieres Winter	Lamara	1.75
Bulgarian	Lean	2.25

VAUGHAN'S ALL SEASONS.

LETTUCE.

CURLED VARIETIES.	Tel. cipher.	Lb.	100 lbs.
Black-Seeded Simpson, very choice	Landman	$0.45	$40.00
Black-Seeded Simpson, selected stock	Landing	.50	45.00
Grand Rapids Forcing	Leggin	.45	40.00
Grand Rapids Forcing, select	Lelwer	.60	55.00
Early Curled Silesia	Laughter	.45	40.00
Early Curled Simpson	Laxity	.45	40.00
The Morse	Likely	.50	45.00
Tilton's White Star	Logline	.45	40.00
CABBAGE AND HEAD VARIETIES.			
All Seasons, Vaughan's	Lordship	.55	50.00
May King, very early	Lassie	.55	50.00
Golden Queen	Lecture	.55	50.00
Big Boston, extra selected	Lanchup	.60	55.00
Black Seeded Tennis Ball	Lodgment	.45	40.00
Blonde Beauty	Landmark	.50	45.00
Brown Dutch Cabbage	Landking	.45	40.00
Buttercup	Lapidist	.45	40.00
California Cream Butter	Lapstone	.50	45.00
Deacon, heads large and solid	Latchet	.50	45.00
Denver Market Forcing	Lattice	.55	50.00
Giant **Crystal Head**	Lectern	.60	
Giant **Glacier**	Legal	.50	
Iceberg	Lesson	.50	45.00
Improved Hanson, very large firm heads	Levant	.50	45.00
Mammoth Black-Seeded Butter	Lintman	.60	55.00
Maximum	Lintel	.50	45.00
New York	Limbo	.55	50.00
Perpignan, or Defiance Summer	Latin	.50	45.00
Prizehead	Linstock	.50	45.00
St. Louis Butterhead, very fancy strain	Livery	.55	50.00
Salamander	Loadstar	.50	45.00
Unrivalled	Levity	.60	55.00
White Cabbage, good head lettuce	Luxury	.55	50.00
Tennis Ball White Seed (Boston Market)	Luthern	.50	45.00
Paris White Cos	Lineal	.50	45.00
Trianon Cos	Logman	.55	50.00
Express Cos	Loger	.60	55.00

PAUL ROSE. HOODOO.

MUSK MELON.

We call special attention to our extra selected stocks of Musk Melons. Our seed is raised by seed growers of reputation and experience and can be depended upon in every respect.

	Tel. cipher.	Lb.	100 lbs.
HOODOO. Introducer's Strain	Mazin	$1.50	
Hoodoo, regular stock	Mazel	.55	50.00
PAUL ROSE. (Petoskey.)			
Vaughan's Select Stock	Maxmillian	1.50	
Regular stock	Maxoka	.55	50.00
THE OSAGE, True			
Stock Seed (Michigan grown)	Mayport	1.40	130.00
Regular Stock, raised from stock seed	Maypole	.60	55.00
Chicago Market Nutmeg	Maming	.65	60.00
Netted Gem, round, choice stock	Malignent	.45	40.00
Netted Gem, oval, choice stock	Malu	.45	40.00
Netted Gem Rocky Ford, choice	Makkat	.50	45.00
Netted Gem Rocky Ford, select	Malady	1.25	
Emerald Gem, one of the sweetest	Mallard	.75	70.00
Tip Top, a very fine market melon	Melody	.55	50.00
Extra Early Nutmeg or Early Citron	Mamma	.55	50.00
Champion Market	Maihem	.55	50.00
Osage Gem	Magian	.65	60.00
Landreth's Early Citron	Maligner	.50	45.00
Lemon	Mansion	.55	50.00
Improved Jenny Lind, selected seed	Marker	.55	50.00
Hackensack	Marmoset	.50	45.00
Extra Early Hackensack, best strain	Maniple	.50	45.00
Montreal Market Nutmeg, very large	Matry	.65	60.00
Banana	Madman	.65	60.00
The Syracuse	Malod	.60	55.00
Vaughan's Improved Milwaukee Market	Malison	1.25	
MANGO MELON, or Vegetable Orange	Mortar	.75	70.00
MARTYNIA Proboscidea	Maccab	1.25	
MUSTARD.			
White London	Mower	.15	12.00
Brown	Mordant	.18	15.00
Chinese, or Giant Southern, curled	Morion	.20	18.00

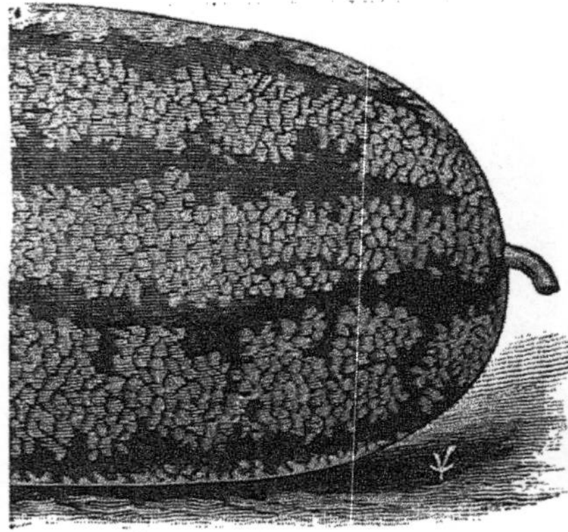

MCIVER'S WONDERFUL SUGAR MELON.

COLES'S EARLY.

WATER MELON.

	Tel. cipher.	Lb.	100 lbs.
Alabama Sweet, select	Mercet	$0.40	$35.00
Black Diamond, original stock	Mercenary	.30	25.00
Chilian	May	.75	
Citron, red-seeded	Messenger	.40	35.00
Colorado Citron	Meteor	.40	35.00
Cole's Early, earliest and very sweet	Messmate	.35	30.00
Cuban Queen	Meter	.35	30.00
Dark Icing	Methodic	.30	25.00
Dixie	Metrop	.30	25.00
Duke Jones	Metropolis	.30	25.00
Early Fordhook	Midland	.35	30.00
Florida Favorite	Midday	.35	30.00
Gipsy Striped, or Rattlesnake	Monotone	.30	25.00
Gray Monarch, or Long White Icing	Mild	.30	25.00
Jones' Jumbo	Miseed	.30	25.00
Kleckley's Sweet	Mislaid	.35	30.00
Kolb's Gem, Improved	Missionary	.30	25.00
McIver's Sugar, the sweetest of all	More	.30	25.00
Peerless, or Ice Cream	Mogul	.35	30.00
Phinney's Improved	Molehill	.30	25.00
Sweetheart	Moodiness	.30	25.00
Triumph	Moon	.30	25.00
Iceberg	Mewing	.30	25.00
Mountain Sweet	Mewry	.35	30.00
Winter, New	Mewter	.65	
Tom Watson	Mezel	.45	40.00

MUSHROOM SPAWN.—Write for quotation on 1,000 lbs. and upwards. We receive from 6 to 8 importations a year.

Pure Culture American Spawn.

Standard Brick, all varieties, per brick, 20c, 100 bricks, $10.00, f. o. b. Chicago; f. o. b. New York, 100 bricks, $10.50 .... Mummy

Direct Brick, all varieties, per brick, 25c; 100 bricks, $13.00, f. o. b. Chicago; f. o. b. New York, 100 bricks, $13.50 .... Mummer

English, per lb., 12c; 10 lbs., $1.00; 100 lbs., $6.00; 1,000 lbs., $55.00 f. o. b. Chicago .... Mumming

100 lbs., $5.50; 1,000 lbs., $50.00 f. o. b. New York..........

French, loose, per lb., 25c.; 2 lb. box, 65c Mural ......

VAUGHAN'S SELECT OHIO YELLOW GLOBE.

ONION.

ONIONS. Write for special quantity prices.

	Tel. cipher.	Lb.	100 lbs.
Large Red Wethersfield	Ominous	$0.75	$65.00
Southport Large Red Globe	Oracle	1.60	150.00
Southport Large Red Globe, Eastern	Obvious	2.00	185.00
Southport Large Yellow Globe	Oral	1.50	140.00
Southport Large Yellow Globe, Eastern	Owcho	1.75	165.00
Southport White Globe	Ouch	1.75	165.00
Ideal White Globe, Eastern grown	Ordanox	2.50	240.00
Ailsa Craig	Osting	5.00	
Australian Brown, Flat	Outgest	.75	65.00
Australian Brown, Globe shaped	Overum	.90	80.00
Bermuda White (True Teneriffe)	Ouger	2.25	200.00
Bermuda Red Teneriffe	Ought	1.50	125.00
Crystal White Wax	Ouken	Sold	out
Bolton (For Sets)	Otter	.75	65.00
Extra Early Flat Red, Eastern grown	Oddity	.80	75.00
Early Flat Yellow Danvers	Obtase	.80	75.00
Giant Brown Rocca	Orthofoc	1.25	110.00
Giant Yellow Rocca or Spanish King	Orstock	1.25	110.00
Mammoth Silver King	Orpherate	1.25	110.00
Ohio Yellow Globe, Ohio grown	Ohope	1.75	165.00
Ohio Red Globe	Onslaught	1.75	160.00
Prizetaker or Mammoth Yellow Spanish	Oppose	.90	80.00
Vaughan's "Apple Shaped" Red Globe	Obliging	1.75	160.00
Vaughan's Pickling	Ordinal	1.60	150.00
White Barletta	Oavking	1.35	125.00
White Queen	Ovek	1.35	125.00
White Portugal or Silver Skin	Ouchat	1.25	115.00
White Welsh	Overall	1.50	
Yellow Cracker, very choice	Obtrude	.85	75.00
Yellow Globe Danvers	Outing	1.25	115.00
Fancy Yellow Globe	Onward	1.40	130.00
Yellow Strasburg or Yellow Dutch	Outil	.75	70.00

ONION SETS.

We mail samples and quote lowest prices on application.

White Multiplier Sets	Owaken.	Shallots	Owabut.
White Bottom Sets	Owack.	Egyptian, Winter top sets	Ovupt.
Yellow Bottom Sets	Owaf.	Red Summer top sets	Owank.
Red Bottom Sets	Owaking.	Yellow Potato	Ollace.

Bbls. extra, 25c. Bags at cost.

OKRA.

		Lb.	100 lbs.
White Velvet	Oblate	$0.20	$18.00
Dwarf	Oasis	.20	18.00
Tall, Perkin's **Mammoth**	Obese	.20	18.00

VAUGHAN'S CHAMPION MOSS CURLED PARSLEY.

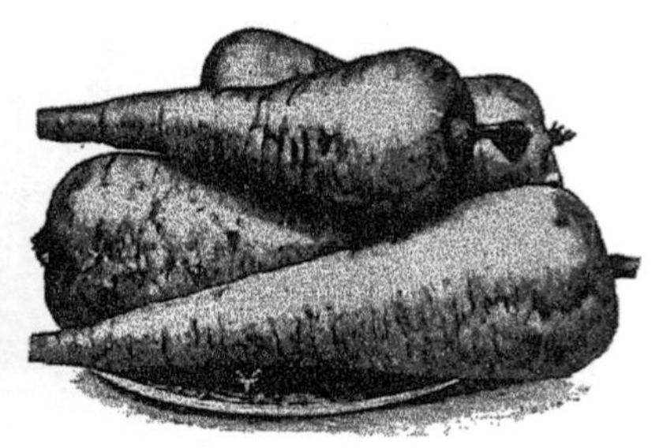

MAGNUM BONUM PARSNIP.

	Tel. cipher.	Lb.	100 lbs.
PARSLEY. (Short Crop)			
Vaughan's Champion Moss Curled	Pacify	$0.75	
Double Curled	Packstaff	.85	
Fern Leaved	Paci	.75	
Plain	Planeness	.75	
Rooted Hamburg	Pala	.75	
Vaughan's XXX	Pake	1.00	
PARSNIP. (Short Crop)			
Long Smooth, or Abbott's Hollow Crown	Palmpaid	.35	30.00
Improved Guernsey, smooth, fine grain	Pallor	.35	30.00
Magnum Bonum	Pamara	.35	30.00
Vaughan's Marrowfat	Petty	.45	40.00
Vaughan's Intermediate	Peter	.55	50.00

PEAS.

		Bush.
Alaska	Pant	$5.50
Alderman	Peaceful	6.00
Advancer	Pedestal	6.00
American Wonder, Bliss'	Pantaloon	6.00
Black Eyed Marrowfat	Pantomime	4.00
Champion of England	Parent	6.00
Dwarf Defiance	Paret	6.50
Dwarf Grey Sugar	Perigraph	7.00
Dwarf Telephone, or Daisy (extra choice)	Pemphone	6.50
Extra Early Premium Gem, or Little Gem	Passport	6.25
Everbearing	Partisan	5.50
First and Best	Pasturage	5.25
Gradus	Penant	7.50
Heroine, one of the best Second Earlies	Paver	6.00
Horsford's Market Garden	Pavillion	6.00
Juno	Pav	6.00
Laxtonian	Pavline	8.00
Little Marvel	Pax	7.50
Long Island Mammoth	Pedantry	6.00
Maud S., true stock	Peorea	5.50
Melting Sugar	Peristyle	Crop failed
Nott's Excelsior, one of the best earlies	Pella	6.00
Pride of the Market	Penchiant	7.00
Stratagem, Improved	Percolate	6.00
Surprise, fine extra early	Penult	6.50
Sutton's Excelsior	Peart	7.50
Telephone, regular stock	Perfidius	6.00
Telephone, Vaughan's Improved	Perfid	6.50
Thomas Laxton	Pealing	7.50
Vaughan's Sweet Market	Premptory	Failure
Velocity	Pezel	6.50
White Marrowfat, large	Perk	4.00
Witham Wonder	Peasantry	Out
Yorkshire Hero	Pergolt	5.50
Canada Field. Closest market price		

Write for prices on items not quoted.

PEPPER.

	Tel. cipher.	Lb.
Magnum Dulce, the largest	Perm	$3.00
Vaughan's Improved Sweet Mountain	Picaroon	1.10
Large Bell or Bullnose	Peste	1.10
Neapolitan	Petrella	1.25
Cayenne, long red	Persevere	1.25
Celestial, select stock	Personage	1.25
Chinese Giant	Perplexity	2.50
Golden Dawn	Perusal	1.25
Elephant's Trunk	Pertinacious.	1.25
Mammoth Golden Queen	Peremptory	1.25
Red Cherry	Physician	1.25
Red Cluster	Physial	1.25
Red Chili	Pepita	1.25
Ruby King	Pianist	1.10
Spanish Monstrous	Pibroch	1.25
Upright Salad	Pedro	2.50
Cayenne Pickling	Permeate	1.25
Tabasco	Perpure	3.00

SWEET POTATOES. (3 barrel lots, 25c. less).
Prices subject to change. Quotations given.

Yellows	Phylon	....
Reds, will be scarce again	Phyllis	....
The African Bunch Yam (Vineless)	Phylas	....

SEED POTATOES.—Northern Grown.
Prices subject to change.

Our potatoes are grown especially for us from our stock seed under contract, and are true to name, selected as to size and shape. Barrel contains 11 pecks. (No charge for bbls.) We have a good stock of the following which we own at right prices. Prices vary with the market. We will quote by mail upon request.

	Tel. cipher.	Bu.	Bbls.
Vaughan's White Ohio, early	Pinnac		
Nebraska, fine, late	Prince		
Gold Coin, medium	Protensia		
Acme	Potshard		
Carman No. 3, late	Pilloree		
Irish Cobbler, good, early	Picobbler		
Hewes' Early	Pitpat		
Vaughan's Improved Early Ohio, fancy	Pinnacle		
Rural New Yorker No. 2, late	Plexus		
Sir Walter Raleigh, late	Raleigh		
White Triumph, or Pride of the South	Plumola		
Red Triumph	Pistach		

PUMPKIN.		Lb.	100 lbs.
Winter Queen, or Winter Luxury	Postrn	$0.45	$40.00
Vaughan's Mammoth Prize	Pondag	.70	65.00
Calhoun	Polyram	.40	35.00
Golden Oblong	Ponifer	.40	35.00
Japanese Pie	Pompilo	.50	45.00
Large Cheese	Pondal	.35	30.00
Large Field (Connecticut)	Polymp	.18	17.00
Large Tours, or Mammoth French	Ponert	.45	40.00
Quaker Pie	Portley	.45	40.00
Small Sugar	Portens	.30	25.00
Sweet Potato	Poser	.50	45.00
Cushaw, Striped, or White	Poten	.55	

RHUBARB.

Linnaeus	Rejoin	.80	75.00
Mammoth	Rejoice	.80	

ROOTS. We have a fine stock. Write for special prices.

VAUGHAN'S SCARLET GLOBE.

In comparing prices customers must bear in mind that our Radish Seed is raised from selected transplanted roots.

RADISH.	Tel. cipher.	Lb.	100 lbs.
All Seasons	Rabble	$0.35	$30.00
Cincinnati Market, long Scarlet	Raisen	.30	25.00
Crimson Giant Forcing	Radiate	.40	35.00
Earliest Carmine Turnip, Vaughan's	Ramoose	.35	30.00
Early Scarlet Turnip, White Tip Forcing	Ranter	.40	35.00
Earliest White Olive-shaped	Radix	.40	35.00
Earliest White Turnip (short leaved)	Raven	.35	30.00
Early Scarlet Globe, Vaughan's Select	Ratsbane	.40	35.00
Early Scarlet Globe, Ordinary	Ratooner	.30	25.00
Early Deep Scarlet Turnip	Rancer	.35	30.00
Early Scarlet Globe, White Tip Forcing (Scarlet Turnip, White Tip Forcing)	Reggy	.40	35.00
Early Long Scarlet (short top)	Rapacious	.35	30.00
Early White Giant Stuttgart	Reform	.35	30.00
French Breakfast	Rayful	.35	30.00
French Breakfast, Improved	Readjust	.45	40.00
Golden Yellow Summer	Raysop	.35	30.00
Half Long Deep Scarlet	Reach	.35	30.00
Improved Chartier	Reading	.35	30.00
Long Brightest Scarlet, white tip (Cardinal)	Realley	.35	30.00
Long White Strassburg	Reaping	.35	30.00
Long White Vienna or Lady Finger	Reapting	.35	30.00
Non Plus Ultra	Rebuff	.40	35.00
Olive Deep Scarlet Short Top (20 days) forcing	Refine	.45	40.00
Olive Shaped Deep Scarlet	Rebuke	.40	35.00
Oval Yellow May	Redeam	.35	30.00
Scarlet Turnip, White Tip (select)	Reclaim	.35	30.00
Triumph, scarlet and white	Reanol	.40	35.00
Vaughan's Market, long white	Rand	.35	30.00
Vaughan's Cardinal Forcing	Random	.45	40.00
Wood's Early Frame	Regrste	.35	30.00
White Icicle, the earliest long white	Reacting	.35	30.00
Winter Varieties.			
Chinese Mammoth or Celestial	Raiment	.40	35.00
California Mammoth White Winter	Regan	.40	35.00
Half Long Black Winter	Rent	.40	35.00
Long White Spanish	Renter	.40	35.00
Long Black Spanish	Reality	.35	30.00
Osaka	Repeat	.35	30.00
Rose, or **Scarlet China Winter**	Reckless	.35	30.00
Round Black Spanish	Reclose	.35	30.00
Munich	Ranting	.40	35.00
Sakurajima	Repent	1.00	

	Tel. cipher.	Lb.	100 lbs.
SALSIFY.			
Mammoth Sandwich Island	Sacker	$0.55	$50.00
SCORZONERA, or **Black Salsify**	Sacristan	1.25	
SORREL, Broad-Leaved French	Sagacity	1.25	
SPINACH. Write for prices on larger lots.			
Bloomsdale, or Norfolk, Savoy-Leaved	Salem	.12	10.00
Extra Large Round-Leaved	Saltern	.12	10.00
Large Round Viroflay	Saltier	.12	10.00
Long Standing	Sandal	.12	10.00
Prickly Seeded	Sapphire	.12	10.00
Tetragonia, or New Zealand	Sanguine	.35	30.00
Victoria	Satrap	.12	10.00
Vaughan's Triumph	Satrox	.15	13.00
Swiss Chard	Bream	.35	30.00
" " Lucullus	Sappy	.45	40.00
" " Lyon	Saturn	.40	35.00

Chicago Warted Hubbard Squash.

SQUASH.

	Tel. cipher.	Lb.	100 lbs.
Boston Marrow	Saver	$0.40	$35.00
Chicago Warted Hubbard	Scaffold	.55	50.00
Chicago Orange Marrow	Scabbard	.45	40.00
Delicious	Scolder	.55	50.00
Delicata	Scalons	.45	40.00
Essex Hybrid	Schemer	.45	40.00
Early White Bush	Secor	.32	28.00
Early Yellow Bush	Seeker	.32	28.00
Faxon's Brazilian	Schooner	.45	40.00
Fordhook "Bush"	Sermon	.45	40.00
Fordhook Early	Scape	.50	45.00
Giant Summer Crookneck	Scroptic	.45	35.00
Golden Bronze	Scullion	.45	40.00
Golden Hubbard	Scull	.55	50.00
Hubbard, extra select	Scoundrel	.55	50.00
Mammoth White Bush, extra select	Scutcheon	.35	30.00
Mammoth Yellow Bush	Scuttle	.35	30.00
Marblehead	Seborn	.65	60.00
Pike's Peak, or Sibley	Sealegs	.45	40.00
Straight Neck	Scobs	.45	40.00
Vegetable Marrow	Sectary	.50	45.00
White Summer Crookneck	Sedan	.35	30.00
Yellow Summer Crookneck	Secant	.35	30.00

TOBACCO.

	Tel. cipher.	Lb.
Big Havana	Tabard	$2.25
Big Oronoko	Tabby	2.25
Brazilian American	Table	2.75
Comstock's Spanish	Talmud	3.00
Connecticut Seed Leaf	Tabling	2.25
General Grant	Taboret	3.00
Harby	Tape	2.75
Primus	Tally	2.25

NEW STONE.

TOMATO.

All our seed is contract grown by the most reliable and experienced men. It can absolutely be relied upon.

	Tel. cipher.	Lb.	10 lbs.
Vaughan's Earliest of All	Tampa	$1.50	$14.00
Vaughan's Model	Thaning	1.75	
Dwarf Stone, new	Taut	1.75	16.50
Livingston's Globe, new	Tapestry	1.50	14.00
Early Detroit	Taper	1.85	17.50
Atlantic Prize	Tapac	1.40	12.50
Acme	Tapan	1.40	12.50
Beauty	Tarket	1.25	11.50
Bonny Best	Tarry	1.75	16.50
Buckeye State	Tarnish	1.50	14.00
Chalk's Jewel	Taler	1.50	14.00
Coreless	Tatting	1.60	15.00
Cream City	Tampering	1.25	11.50
Crimson Cushion	Tattle	2.25	21.50
Dwarf Aristocrat	Taurine	1.60	15.00
Dwarf Champion	Taurus	1.60	15.00
Earliana	Tauber	1.50	14.00
Early Michigan	Teacher	1.25	11.50
Enormous	Tepesy	1.60	15.00
Favorite	Teeter	1.25	11.50
Freedom	Teg	1.25	11.50
Golden Queen	Templar	1.40	12.50
Hummer	Temser	1.60	15.00
Honor Bright	Tenabrice	1.25	11.50
Imperial	Taxe	1.25	11.50
June Pink	Teber	2.00	19.00
Magnus	Tehama	1.50	14.00
Matchless	Tepid	1.50	14.00
Pear-shaped Yellow	Tapa	1.50	
Pear-shaped Red	Tasop	1.50	
Peach Red	Thanksgiver	1.50	
Peach Yellow	Thoral	1.50	
Plum Yellow	Thrall	1.50	
Plum Red	Testatrix	1.50	
Perfection	Testaning	1.25	11.50
Ponderosa	Testudo	2.25	21.50
Stone, Improved	Thesis	1.25	11.50
Trophy	Theocrat	1.25	11.50
Red Cherry	Texual	1.50	
Tall Champion	Taural	1.75	
Ground Cherry (Yellow Husk)	Temptation	1.50	

Tomato Forcing Sorts.	Tel. cipher.	Lb.	10 lbs.
Frogmore, selected	Teheram	$2.00	$19.00
Hubert's Marvel	Tekter	2.00	
Carter's Sunrise	Teralt	2.00	
Comet	Telner	2.50	
Lorillard	Teporal	2.00	19.00
Sterling Castle	Temal	2.00	
Sutton's Best forcing	Theo	2.00	
TURNIP.			100 lbs.
Early White Milan	Tipsy	.75	70.00
Extra Early Purple Top Milan	Tibing	.70	65.00
Purple Top Strap Leaf, choice	Thugord	.28	25.00
Purple Top White Globe	Tirode	.30	28.00
White Egg	Token	.30	28.00
Large White Norfolk	Timely	.25	22.00
White Flat Dutch	Thumper	.25	22.00
Yellow Aberdeen	Tooling	.25	22.00
Sweet German	Togated	.30	28.00
Golden Ball	Tidiness	.25	22.00
Long Cowhorn	Throng	.32	30.00
Amber Globe	Thrice	.25	22.00
Seven Top	Titmouse	.25	22.00
Snowball	Tonsotial	.28	25.00
Rhode Island Rock	Tonsure	.40	
Yellow Stone	Three	.30	28.00
Teltow	Tomer	.35	30.00
SWEDES OR RUTABAGAS.			
Monarch	Thorn	.22	20.00
Laing's Swede	Torsion	.22	20.00
Carter's Improved Swede	Topmed	.22	20.00
Vaughan's Imp. American, Purple top	Topic	.25	23.00
Skirving's	Toward	.24	21.00
Sutton's Champion, extra fine	Tracking	.25	22.00
Breadstone	Thriff	.25	22.00
White Swede	Tramper	.22	20.00
Vassar	Trading	.28	25.00

FARM and MISCELLANEOUS SEEDS.

Prices Change; write for latest quotations. Bags Extra. Terms Cash.

Items with * F. O. B. New York or Chicago. Balance of list F. O. B. Chicago. Ask our New York House for Quotations. Items with no prices attached are subject to quick market changes. Latest quotations on application.

	Tel. ciph.	Lb.	100 lbs.	Bu.
Barley, Success 48 lbs. to the bushel	Wolf			
Barley, White Hulless, Montana grown	Woland			
Barley, Mansury, 48 lbs. to the bushel	Wollab			
*Beggar Weed, Giant	Beggar			
*Bromus Inermis	Warouse			
Broom Corn, Improved Evergreen	Whistlan			
Buckwheat Japanese, write for prices	Bucking			
Buckwheat Silver Hull, write for prices	Buckram			
Chufas	Woodcut	.15	12.00	
Corn, Kaffir, White	Wobweb			
CORN.—Field (Write for latest prices.)—				
Rhode Island White Cap Flint	Coryph			
Golden Surprise	Coronal			
King Philip, Flint	Coterie			
Longfellow, Flint	Cougar			
Giant Long White, Flint	Cough			
Dewdrop, Flint	Cosecant			
Will's Gehu	Cowmarke			
Hickory King	Corporal			
Leaming	Cotter			
Iowa Gold Mine	Costape			
Iowa Silver Mine	Couple			
Minnesota No. 13	Corner			

CORN, Field—Continued.	Tel. ciph.	Lb.	100 lbs.	Bu.
Pride of the North	Cousin			
Reid's Yellow Dent on the Ear	Cowmuling			
Reid's Yellow Dent shelled	Cowhide			
Silver **King** (Wisconsin No. 7)	Coulter			
Boone County White Dent	Coward			
Madison Yellow Dent, Best early	Cort			
Sunshine Dent, Earliest	Corner			
CORN—Pop, all selected ears for seed.				
Mapledale Prolific	Crater	$0.05	$4.00	
Queen's Golden	Craven	.05	4.00	
White Rice	Crawdart	.05	4.00	
Illinois Snowball	Crasher	.05	4.00	
Cow Peas, Michigan Favorite	Witator			
Cow Peas, Black-Eye	Witation	At market price		
Cow Peas, Whippoorwill	Witric	At market price		
Cow Peas, Mixed	Witrock	At market price		

		Lb.	100 lbs
Espersette, or Sainfoin	Witwell	.14	
Flax Seed, write for prices	Witword		
Giant Spurry	Woffle		
Lupins, Yellow	Woctile	.07	6.50
Maw, blue	Whigol	.18	
Milo Maize, White	Whimney		
Millet, Pearl or Cat Tail	Wood		
Oats, Black Tartarian	Womate		
Swedish	Wome		
Lincoln	Womedy		
Winter Turf	Womegal		
Peas, Canada Field, write for prices	Parasite		
*Peanuts, Spanish	Pandote	.09	
*Peanuts, Mammoth Virginia	Pandave	.09	
***Rape,** Essex	Wodif		
Salt Bush, Australian	Woodcock	.90	
Sand Vetch	Woffer	.12	11.00
Soja Beans	Busk		
Speltz	Speltz		
Sugar Cane, Early Amber	Whisk		
***Sunflower,** Mammoth Russian	Whough		
Teosinte	Wogen	1.25	
Velvet Bean	Velvet		
*VETCHES, Spring	Wognate		4.25
WHEAT, Dawson's Golden Chaff	Wool		
WHEAT, Defiance, Turkish Red	Woolman		
WHEAT, Mealy Winter	Woolly		
WHEAT, Blue Stem	Woolsack		
WHEAT, Macaroni	Woolweb	Write for prices	
WHEAT, Saskatchewan Fife	Woolwoven		
*WINTER RYE	Wompart		
WILD RICE	Whapter		

TREE SEEDS

	Tel. cipher.	Lb.	100 lbs.
* Ash, White	Wondem	$0.25	$20.00
* Box Elder	Wonduct	.25	20.00
* Catalpa Speciosa. True	Wonfall	2.75	
* Locust, Honey	Wonfront	.40	35.00
* Locust, Black or Yellow	Wonform	.40	35.00
* Maple, Oregon Mammoth	Won	1.10	
* Osage Orange	Wongins	.45	

ALL GRASS AND CLOVER SEEDS.—Alfalfa, Alsyke, White Clover, Crimson, Medium Red, and Mammoth Clover, etc. Prices on application.

VAUGHAN'S

Trade List of Flower Seeds.

"THE BEST FLOWER SEEDS IN AMERICA."

Our list contains all the best novelties that we know to be worthy of cultivation and that are improvements on the older kinds or entirely new varieties, as well as all the standard sorts. The quality of our seeds is the very best, and our prices are reasonable.

☞Quantities of ¼ lb. and over are charged at the pound rates (⅛ lbs. at the oz. rate), ½ ozs. at the oz. rate, but only when the price per ounce is 60c., or more, and is not otherwise quoted.

We do not sell half ounces where the price per ounce is 15c or under.

	TEL. CIPHER.	OZ.	LB.
Abobra Viridiflora, Ornamental Cucumber	Abapo	$0.40	
Abronia Umbellata Grandiflora	Abas	.20	$2.20
Arenaria	Abandon	.80	
Abrus Precatorius (Weather Plant)	Abatable	.25	2.25
Abutilon, fine mixed ... per ⅛ oz., 25c.	Abavus	1.60	
New Hybrids, mixed ... per ⅛ oz., 50c.	Abba	3.00	
Acacia Lophanta Speciosa Compacta	Abdera	.10	1.00
Mixed, many kinds	Abderita	.10	1.00
Acanthus Latifolius, very decorative	Abdite	.10	.70
Mollis, fine foliage	Abdix	.10	1.20
Achillea. The Pearl, very fine ... ⅛ oz., 30c.	Abditery	2.00	
Aconitum Napellus, Monk's Hood, blue	Abdo	.45	5.00
Napellus Flore Albo, white	Abdodge	1.40	
Acroclinium Roseum, pink	Abdomen	.10	.90
Roseum Flore Albo, white	Abduco	.10	.80
Roseum mixed	Abductus	.10	.80
Adenophora Potaninii	Aberrant	.60	
Adlumia Cirrhosa, Allegheny Vine	Abeo	2.80	
Adonis Aestivalis, (Flos Adonis), red	Aberro	.10	.35
Autumnalis, red	Abfore	.10	.35
Vernalis, bright yellow	Abgabion	.30	
Agapanthus Umbellatus	Abjellant	.40	
Agathaea Coelestis (Amelloides), Blue Daisy	Abhor	.60	
Ageratum Mexicanum, blue	Abiga	.10	1.20
Mexicanum Album, White	Abitio	.10	1.20
Nanum Luteum, yellow	Abitiory	.20	
Imperial Dwarf Blue	Abitus	.20	2.20
Imperial Dwarf White	Abject	.20	2.20
Blue Perfection	Abjecter	.25	2.25
Little Blue Star, splendid novelty, ¼ oz., $1.00	Abjig		
Princess Victoria Louise	Abjection	.20	2.00
Mixed	Abjicio	.10	1.00
Lasseauxi, pink	Abjectness	.30	
Agrostemma Coeli Rosa	Abjuro	.10	.80
Coronaria, mixed	Ablatus	.10	1.20
Flos Jovis, rose	Ablego	.10	1.20
Alonsoa Grandiflora	Ablick	.15	
Warscewiczi	Ablickator	.15	
Alyssum Maritimum, Sweet Alyssum . 10 lbs., $8.50	Ablutto	.10	1.00
Benthami Compactum Erectum, dwarf	Ablutus	.20	2.20
Vaughan's Little Gem, extra fine strain	Abnego	.50	6.00
Saxatile Compactum, Gold Dust, hardy peren.	Abnota	.15	1.65

	TEL. CIPHER.	OZ.	LB.
Amaranthus Tricolor, Joseph's Coat	Abuuo	$0.10	$1.15
Tricolor Splendens	Abode	.30	3.50
Atropurpureus	Abolea	.10	.30
Caudatus (Love Lies Bleeding), red	Abolitus	.10	.30
Superbus (Coleus-leaved)	Abolia	.10	.60
Salicifolius (Willow-leaved)	Abania	.30	3.00
Many sorts mixed	Abord	.10	.30
Ambrosia Mexicana	Aborior	.20	2.00
Ammobium Alatum Grandiflorum	Abrumes	.10	.70
Ampelopsis Veitchi, Boston Ivy	Abrupt	.10	1.35
Anagallis Grandiflora, mixed	Abrus	.25	
Grandiflora Coerulea	Abruption	.35	
Anchusa Angustifolia	Abrutir	.20	2.00
Capensis	Absay	.20	2.00
Capensis Dropmore Variety	Abscessop	1.25	
Anemone Coronaria, mixed	Absell	.25	3.00
Sylvestris	Absentee	1.00	
St. Brigid, large handsome flowers	Abshead	1.20	
Pulsatilla, violet lilac	Abside	1.00	
Anthemis Tinctoria	Absence	.50	
Kelwayi, yellow	Absend	.30	
Antigonon Leptopus, Mountain Rose	Absentia	.25	2.50
Antirrhinum, Large-flowering, choice mixed	Absoof	.20	2.20
Large-flowering, pure white	Abscondo	.30	3.00
" Crescia, deep scarlet	Absconce	.30	3.50
" Firefly, scarlet, white throat	Abscons	.30	3.00
" Golden King, yellow	Absconsus	.30	3.20
" Queen Victoria, large pure white	Abscondit	.35	3.50
" Brilliant, scarlet	Abscond	.30	3.50
" Rose	Abscondy	.40	4.00
" Striped Varieties, mixed	Abscise	.30	3.00
" Venus, beautiful light pink, ¼ oz., $1.00	Abscond		
Vaughan's Special Mixture, extra	Abscoo	.40	4.50
Majus, Coral-red	Abscising	.30	3.00
" White with pink lip	Abscissa	.35	4.00
" Rose (Delicata)	Abscist	.35	4.00
" Many colors mixed	Abscess	.15	1.85
" Nanum "Black Prince"	Abscinde	.35	3.50
" Nanum Queen of the North	Absenter	.30	3.20
" Nanum Dwarf sorts, mixed	Abscord	.20	2.20
" Nanum Albino mixture	Absrated	.60	7.00
" Nanum Aurora	Absrating	.35	3.50
" Nanum Golden Queen	Absrat	.35	3.50
Tom-Thumb, many colors mixed	Abscoon	.35	4.00
" " Snow Queen	Absent	1.20	
Aquilegia, Columbine, Single mixed	Absillio	.15	1.60
Double mixed	Absoloo	.15	1.40
Canadensis, scarlet and yellow	Absolute	.60	7.00
Chrysantha yellow	Absolution	.65	8.00
Chrysantha Grandiflora Alba, white	Absone	1.40	
Chrysantha Fl., pl., double	Absorb	.70	
Helenae, new, very fine	Absopar	1.80	
Improved Long Spurred English Varieties	Absurde	1.00	
Vulgaris Alba Plena, double white	Absorbeo	.30	3.00
Coerulea, blue, Rocky Mt. Columbine	Absorbing	1.00	12.00
Coerulea "Rose Queen" ⅛ oz., 75c.	Absolve	5.00	
Coerulea Hybrida (Haylodgensis)	Absorption	.90	12.00
Nivea Grandiflora	Absondre	.15	1.40
Rose and Scarlet Shades ⅛ oz., 60c.	Absorp		
Vervaeneana Atroviolacea Plenissima	Absumere		
Vaughan's Special Mixture	Abstain	1.50	
Arabis Alpina, white, dwarf	Absum	.30	3.00
Arctotis Grandis, The African Lilac Daisy	Absurdity	.20	2.20
Ardisia, Crenulata 100 seeds, 60c.	Absurdness		

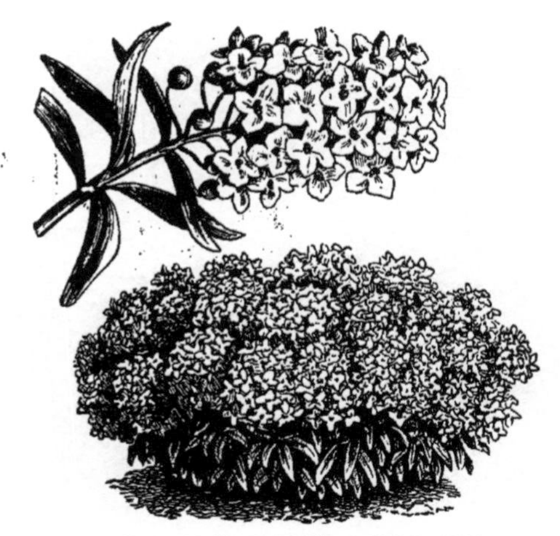

ALYSSUM VAUGHAN'S LITTLE GEM.

	TEL. CIPHER.	OZ.	LB.
Aristolochia Sipho, Dutchman's Pipe	Absusting	$0.80	$10.00
Armeria Maritima, rose	Absusto	.70	
Formosa, red	Abtan	.40	
Artemisia Annua, very decorative	Abthus	.10	.40
Sacrorum, Summer Fir, new... 1/8 oz., $1.00	Abuate		
Asclepias Tuberosa, orange, fine hardy perennial	Abullot	.80	

ASPARAGUS.

	TEL. CIPHER.	OZ.	LB.
Asparagus Plumosus Nanus, Northern Greenhouse Grown, 1,000 seeds at $3.50 per thousand; 5,000 to 10,000 seeds at $3.25 per thousand; 11,000 to 25,000 seeds at $3.00 per thousand; 26,000 to 50,000 seeds at $2.75 per thousand;	Abunde		
Sprengeri, 1,000 seeds, 50c; 100 seeds, 15c	Abusive	.30	4.00
Asparagus Hatcherii............$9.00 per 1,000	Aburria		
Asperula Azurea Setosa	Arcanum	.10	.35
Odorata, Waldmeister, or Sweet Woodruff	Acbarus	.50	6.00

ASTERS.

Our Aster seed is raised by experienced and reliable seed growers, in many cases from our own stock seed and should not be compared with stock raised in the south or by experimenters who use no care and lack experience.

We have divided our list of Aster seed into three sections, arranged according to height. Each section is cataloged alphabetically. The separate sorts of all the varieties are listed according to the established color classification, beginning with white and running through yellow, light pink to dark red and light blue to purple.

DWARF SECTION, up to 10 inch.

	TEL. CIPHER.	OZ.	LB.
Vaughan's Little Gem, height 6 inches, flowers pink and white	Affair	$1.50	
Vaughan's Fireball, a splendid dwarf Aster	Agast	2.00	
Vaughan's Snowball, the best dwarf white Aster	Agastria	1.50	

ASTER QUEEN OF THE MARKET

DWARF SECTION—Continued.

DWARF CHRYSANTHEMUM FLOWERED ASTER.

	TEL. CIPHER.
White	Afier.
White, turning to rose	Afloat.
Peachblossom	Agalman.
Brilliant Rose	Afric.
Crimson	Afront.
Fiery Scarlet..oz. $2.00.	Aftaba.
White, turning to azure-blue	Afoot.
Light Blue and White	Again.
Light Blue	Agalma.
Azure Blue	Afraid.
Dark Blue	Afresh.

Each of above, except noted, per ¼ oz., 35c; per oz., $1.25.

	TEL. CIPHER.	OZ.	LB.
Dwarf Chrysanthemum-Flowered, all colors mixed.	Agaric	$1.00	$14.00

DWARF QUEEN ASTER.

	TEL. CIPHER.
White	Agatine.
Pink	Agitate.
Brilliant Rose	Agitator.
Crimson	Age.
Light Blue	Aging.
Dark Blue	Agitable.

Each of the above, per oz., $1.25.

	TEL. CIPHER.	OZ.	LB.
Dwarf Queen, all colors mixed	Agitation	$0.90	$12.00
Early Flowering Dwarf, all colors mixed	Agleem	.75	9.00
Gloria or Button-hole. The flowers are about 2 inches in diameter, pure white with a scarlet margin	Acting	2.00	
Pigmy, Dwarf Bouquet or Boltze's, mixed, extra choice	Aflight	.85	10.00
Triumph Aster, White	Agleamer	3.00	
" " Crimson	Agleamit	3.50	
" " Scarlet	Aglem	3.00	
" Coppery Scarlet	Agleamio	3.50	
" Deep Violet	Agleamy	3.00	
" Mixed, many colors	Aglee	2.00	

SEMI-TALL SECTION, 11 inches to 16 inches.

COMET ASTER.

	TEL. CIPHER.		TEL. CIPHER.
White	Adjourn.	Carmine	Adjusted.
Bridesmaid, white turning to lilac rose	Adieu.	**Deep Scarlet**	Adjust.
Peach Blossom	Adjunct.	White and Lilac	Adjuster.
Pink, bordered white	Adjudge.	Light Blue and White	Adjure.
Dark Rose	Adjournal.	**Light Blue**	Adjugate.
		Dark Blue	Adjustant.

Each of above, per oz., $1.00.

	TEL. CIPHER.	OZ.	LB.
Comet, all colors **mixed (German Grown)**	Adjustria	$0.65	$8.00
Daybreak Purity, white	Affide	1.00	14.00
" pink, fine for pots	Affianze	.90	12.00

GIANT COMET ASTER.

	TEL. CIPHER.		TEL. CIPHER.
White	Ado.	**Rose**	Adobe.
The Bride, white turning to pink	Adopt.	**Bright Carmine**	Adoctin.
Queen of Spain, soft yellow turning to flesh	Adopting.	Crimson	Adobinger.
Sulphur Yellow	Adog.	**Lavender**	Adobar.
Salmon Rose	Adoar.	**Light Blue**	Adonia.
		Dark Blue	Adopted.

Any of the above, per oz., $1.40; lb., $20.00.

	TEL. CIPHER.	OZ.	LB.
Giant Comet Aster, all colors mixed	Adoptif	$0.90	$12.00
June Flowering White		1.50	
Mikado, white	Anchester	.85	10.00
" pink Rochester	Ancested	.85	10.00
Paeony-flowered (Uhland), Mixed	Adlade	.85	10.00

QUEEN OF THE MARKET ASTER.

	TEL. CIPHER.		TEL. CIPHER.
White	Adverse.	Scarlet..oz 60c, lb $6.50	Adversion.
Pink	Adversely.	Light Blue	Adviso.
Crimson. oz 60c, lb $6.50	Advisable.	Dark Blue	Advocate.
Flesh, oz 65c, lb. $8.00	Advising.		

Each of the above (except those marked), per oz., 50c; per lb., $6.00.

	TEL. CIPHER.	OZ.	LB.
Queen of the **Market**, all the above, best **mixed**	Advock	$0.45	$5.00

VICTORIA ASTER, Vaughan's Improved.

	TEL. CIPHER.		TEL. CIPHER.
Snow White	Acutule.	**Bright Scarlet**	Additio.
Miss Roosevelt, yellow turning to flesh	Admittance.	White, turning to azure-blue	Acutus.
Apple Blossom	Adaquo.	Light Blue and White	Adduco.
Bright Rose, tinged white	Adhuc.	**Light Blue**	Adaxint.
Bright Pink	Adhibeo.	**Azure** Blue	Adamus.
Crimson and White	Adight.	Indigo Blue on white ground	Adinole.
Dark Crimson	Adaucto.	**Dark** Blue and White	Adesus.
		Dark Blue	Adelphia.

	TEL. CIPHER.	OZ.	LB.
Many Colors in splen. mix. (German Grown)	Adipous	$1.25	$18.00
Victoria Aster, imp. col., 6 col., each, net, 20c	Aditus		
" " imp. col., 12 col., each, net, 40c	Adition		
Washington or **Jubilee,** white	Adit	1.80	
" " " sulphur-yellow	Adze	2.00	
" " " mixed	Adytum	1.50	

TALL SECTION, 17 inches and upwards.

	Tel. Cipher.	Oz.	Lb.
Vaughan's Beauty, brilliant red	Afferent	$1.50	

BRANCHING OR SEMPLE ASTER.

	Tel. Cipher.	Oz.	Lb.
White	Adoring	$0.45	$5.00
Daybreak Pink	Adorn	.45	5.00
Rose Pink	Adoringly	.45	5.00
Dark Red	Adoteum	$0.50	$5.50
Lavender	Adota	.45	5.00
Purple	Adouber	.50	6.00
Giant Branching, choice mixed	Adoxa	$0.40	$4.50
Branching, Upright White, regular stock	Adreadit	.85	10.00
" " Pink	Adroit	1.25	
" " Purple	Adroitany	1.00	
Branching Comet, White	Adoxeth	.65	8.00
" " Light Pink	Adoxony	.85	10.00
" " Lavender	Adoxsat	.85	10.00
" Rose Pink	Adoxya	.85	10.00

CARLSON OR INVINCIBLE ASTER.

	Tel. Cipher.
White	Acirto.
Daybreak pink	Acider.
Marquis Pink	Actavus.
Lavender	Acme.
Violet Blue	Acnop.

Each of above, oz., $1.00.

	Tel. Cipher.	Oz.	Lb.
Carlson Aster, mixed, the above	Acnus	$0.90	
Crego, White	Actus	1.00	$14.00
" Shell Pink	Actusay	1.00	14.00
" Dark Pink	Actuate	1.00	14.00
Crown or Cocardeau, mixed	Adventure	.90	12.00
Hercules, White	Adventy		

HOHENZOLLERN ASTER.

	Tel. Cipher.
White	Adoret.
Bride, white turning to pink	Adosomer.
Pink	Adoreting.
Brilliant Rose	Adorx.
Bright Salmon Rose	Adorned.
Crimson	Adourner.
Silvery Lilac	Adorus.
Light Blue	Adorvas.
Azure Blue	Adory.

Each of above, oz., $2.50.

	Tel. Cipher.	Oz.	Lb.
Hohenzollern Aster, many colors, mixed	Adoryus	$1.60	$22.00
" " Extra Early, White	Adorneth	1.50	
" " Extra Early, Rose	Adorngly	1.50	
Ostrich Feather, many colors, mixed	Adorare	1.25	18.00
Quilled Sulphur, Yellow	Advance	.60	
Quilled German mixed	Advenir	.30	3.50
Royal Purple	Ancestry	.80	10.00
Smith's Peerless, White	Ancesture	2.50	
Smith's Peerless, Pink	Ancestust	5.00	
Unicum White	Ancestuv	2.00	

BED OF VAUGHAN'S ASTERS

PAEONY-FLOWERED PERFECTION.

	TEL. CIPHER.	OZ.	LB.
Rose and White	Accentric	$1.25	
Snow White	Accensus	1.25	$18.00
Sunlight, sulphur-yellow	Acinose	1.25	
Delicate Rose	Accera	1.80	
Surprise, chamois turning to pink	Acinetan	1.25	
Pink (La Superbe)	Accepso	1.20	17.00
Crimson and White	Achilles	1.40	
Crimson	Accido	1.25	18.00
Brilliant Scarlet	Aceo	1.25	
Gravelotte, Bloodred	Accurbus	1.25	18.00
Sky-Blue and White	Accurbo	1.30	
Light Blue and White	Acesco	1.30	
Amethyst	Achiote	1.25	
Light Blue	Acerbus	1.20	17.00
Azure Blue	Accabot	1.40	
White and Blue-black	Acetum	1.25	
Dark Blue	Accoló	1.20	17.00
Shining Blue-black	Acerbe	1.25	
Imported Collection, 6 colors, each, 17c, net	Acker		
Imported Collection, 12 colors, each, 34c, net	Ackerton		
Paeony-Flowered Perfection, splendid mixture (German Grown)	Acena	1.00	13.00

ASTERS—Continued

	TEL. CIPHER.	OZ.	LB.
Vaughan's Florists' Mixture	Agrippa	$1.00	$14.00
White Tall Varieties, mixed	Agrom	.75	10.00
Dwarf Asters, many classes and colors mixed	Agreet	.50	6.50
Vaughan's Excelsior Mixture of Dwarf Asters. It is comprised of the most distinct and desirable colors of the different classes of Dwarf Asters specially selected for this mixture.	Agricole	1.25	16.00
Tall Asters, many classes and colors mixed	Agreement	.25	3.00

Vaughan's Excelsior Mixture of Tall Asters.
This is a mixture of the most beautiful, striking and distinct colors of the tall growing Asters, selected from the cream of the **Peony Fld. Victoria, Crown, Giant Comet, Hohenzollern, Ostrich Plume, Carlson, Branching** and other desirable sorts, and includes many kinds specially purchased for this mixture. Per oz., $1.25; lb., $16.00. Agrilus.

	TEL. CIPHER.	OZ.	LB.
Single Elegance, White	Agriculat	$1.00	
" " Dark Blue	Agricultna.	1.00	
" " Lavender	Agriculera.	1.00	
Perennial Asters, choice mixed. ¼ oz., 20c.	Ahoy	.65	

	TEL. CIPHER.	OZ.	LB.
Auricula (Primula), fine mixed, ⅛ oz., 60c.	Aulpha	$4.00	
Bachelor's Button, mixed (see also Centaurea)	Cede	.10	$0.60
Balloon Vine (Cardiospermum Halicacabum) 5 lbs., $2.65	Babakoto	.10	.60

BALSAMS—DOUBLE.

	TEL. CIPHER.		TEL. CIPHER.
Crimson	Balatus.	Crimson Spotted	Barbaos.
Flesh	Balneum.	Solferino	Barbula.
Pink	Balteus.	Lilac	Barcae.
Scarlet	Bamballo.	Light Lemon	Barcel.
Double White	Bare.	Dark Blue	Barcine

Each of the above, oz., 30c; lb., $3.00.

	TEL. CIPHER.	OZ.	LB.
Atrosanguinea plenissima, double blood red	Bacenite	$0.30	$ 3.00
Malmaison Pink	Barbus	.40	4.50
Prince Bismarck, salmon rose	Bardl	.45	5.00
Vaughan's Invincible, the best mixture in existence.	Baris	.50	6.00
Alba Perfecta, or white Defiance, best double white.	Beatus	.15	1.25
Double Camellia-Flowered, all colors best mixed	Barium	.25	2.50
Improved Double Camellia-Flowered, choice mxd.	Barnacle	.50	6.00
Double Dwarf, mixed	Baro	.20	2.00
Double Rose-Flowered, best quality mixed	Basilia	.20	2.00
Double Carnation Striped, mixed	Basilicus	.20	2.00
Tall Double, mixed colors 5 lbs., $5.50	Bassaris	.10	1.20
Balsam Apple, (Momordica Balsamina)	Beatus	.15	1.25
" **Pear**, (Momordica Charantia)	Belides	.15	1.40
" **Apple and Pear**, mixed	Begorra	.15	1.30
Baptisia Australis	Benevole	.25	[illegible]
Bartonia Aurea	Bessicus	.15	1.80
Begonia, Single Tuberous Rtd., mx., 1-32 oz., $1.00	Biblus		
Dbl. Tuberous Rtd., mx. pkt. (500 seeds) 17c net.	Bibo		

CALENDULA

CAMPANULA—Canterbury Bells

BEGONIA—Continued.

	TEL. CIPHER.	OZ.	LB.
Erfordia, rosy carmine......1-32 oz., $1.00.	Bibolation		
Semperflorens Alba	Biblical ..	$1.25	
Semperflorens Berna.........1-32 oz., 75c..	Bibsat ...		
Semperflorens **Red Lubeca**..1-32 oz., $2.00..	Bibsute ...		
Semperflorens Mixed	Bibale ...	1.25	
Gracilis Luminosa..........1-32 oz., $1.00..	Bibolate ..		
Gracilis Mignon...........1-64 oz., $2.00..	Bibmat ...		
Rex, extra fine mx. pkt. (500 seeds) 20c net..	Bibola ...		
Vernon, splendid bedding sort, ⅛ oz., 30c..	Bibrax ...	2.00	
Bellis, or Double Daisy, White..................	**Biforous...**	.90	$12.00
Vaughan's Mammoth Mixture... ⅛ oz., 25c..	**Bifrons ...**	**1.50**	
" " **White** ...	Big	1.50	
" " **Pink** .... ⅛ oz., 35c..	Bigamist ..	2.25	
Monstrosa, double white, new..⅛ oz., .60c..	Bigamy ..	4.00	
" " pink, new... ⅛ oz., 60c..	Biggin ..	4.00	
Turban new double red.......1-32 oz., 75c..	Bigbart ...		
Longfellow, double pink..................	Bigam	1.25	18.00
Snowball, double white..................	Bigaroon .	1.25	18.00
Extra Choice Mixed........... ¼ oz., 30c..	Biggen ...	1.20	16.00
Fine Mixed..............................	Bigha	.70	9.00
Betonica Grandiflora Superba..................	Bihart ...	1.25	
Bidens Atrosanguinea, the black Dahlia..........	Bike	.45	
" Dahlioides, new .....per ¼ oz., $1.00....	Bijuary ...		
Bird of Paradise, (Poinciana Gillesi)...........	Bilbo	.30	3.50
Bocconia Japonica.........................	Bilat	.25	2.80
Boltonia Asteroides	Bilamary .	1.20	
" Latisquama	Balamute .	1.50	
Brachycome Iberidifolia, Swan River Daisy, **Blue.**	Bilalo	.40	4.00
" " **White**	Bile	.40	4.00
" " **Pink**	Bilestion ..	.40	4.00
" **Mixed**	Biler	.30	3.20
" " Snow Star...........	Bilcay	1.50	
" " Blue Star...........	Bilcayate .	1.50	
Browallia, mixed..........................	Billiment .	.30	3.50
Speciosa Major, large, blue..1-16 oz., 80c..	**Billions ...**		
Briza maxima	Billiards ..	.10	.80

	TEL. CIPHER.	OZ.	LB
Bryonopsis Laciniosa, fine annual climber	Bilirubin	$0.20	$2.00
Bupthalmium Cordifolium	Bill	.25	
Cacalia, mixed (Tassel Flower)	Caaba	.15	1.50
Calampelis Scaber, a splendid climber	Cabah	.50	
Calandrinia Grandiflora	Caback	.30	
" Umbellata	Cabadate	.60	
Calceolaria Hybrida, finest strain. 1-32 oz., $1.25	Caballero		
Calendula (Pot Marigold). Meteor. 5 lbs., $2.60	Cabasset	.10	.63
Sulphurea Plena, double sulphur-yellow	Cabbish	.10	.70
Prince of Orange 5 lbs., $3.00	Cabble	.10	.70
Grandiflora fl. pl. (Orange King) 5 lbs., $2.60	Cabeca	.10	.60
Pongei fl. pl., double white	Caberea	.10	1.00
Mixed 5 lbs., $2.20	Cabin	.10	.50
California Poppy, see Escholtzia.			
Calliopsis, mixed 5 lbs., $2.75	Cabinet	$0.10	$0.60
Dwarf Sorts, mixed	Cabarian	.10	.80
Double mixed	Cabob	.10	1.00
Lanceolata, golden yellow; perennial	Caboche	.20	2.00
Grandiflora	Cabomba	.20	2.40
Coronata Maxima	Cable	.15	1.80
Hybrida Superba	Cabool	.15	1.80
Drummondi (Golden Wave)	Caboose	.10	.60
Bicolor Nana "Golden Ray"	Cabope	.20	2.00
Radiata, "Tiger Flower"	Cabotle	.20	2.00
Vaughan's Special Mixture	Cabotage	.20	2.00
Callirhoe Involucrata (Verticillata)	Cabat	.40	
Pedata (digita)	Cabinate	.20	
CAMPANULA (Canterbury Bell.)			
Calycanthema, Cup and Saucer, mixed	Cabrank	1.00	14.00
" Pink	Cabrero	1.20	
" White	Cabriole	2.00	
" Striped	Cabriolenr	1.00	
" Blue	Cabstand	1.00	
Medium, Single mixed	Cabure	.15	1.80
" " Blue	Cachum	.20	2.20
" " White	Cacnunba	.25	3.00
" Rose	Cachunc	.25	3.00
" " Striped	Cacooy	.25	3.00
" Double mixed	Cacam	.65	8.00
" Double and Single, mixed	Cachunde	.45	5.00
Macrantha, blue, large flowered	Capud	.20	
Macrostyla, large violet flowers	Cacala	.80	
Mirabilis, beautiful species, 1-32 oz. 80c.	Cacadot		
Speculum (Venus Looking Glass), mixed	Cachou	.10	1.00
Carpatica, Blue (Hair Bell)	Cachuper	.20	2.00
" Alba, White	Cachuping	.25	2.80
Persicifolia Grandiflora Alba (Backhousei)	Cachexia	2.00	
" " Coerulea	Cachination	1.80	
" " Mixed	Cacicat	1.20	
" double white (Moerheimi). ⅛ oz., $1.00	Caclam		
Pyramidalis, Blue	Cachupious	.40	4.50
" Alba, White	Cachupit	.50	
Perennial Varieties, mixed	Cacicus	.35	4.00
Canary Bird Flower, fine climber for shade	Cacis	.10	1.00

CANDYTUFT.

Candytuft. Coronaria. White Rocket, 5 lbs. $1.75	Caco	$0.10	$0.40
Giant Hyacinth-Flowered, White	Cacobo	.15	1.50
Empress, a very choice strain	Cadet	.15	1.50
Crimson, (Umbellata Purpurea)	Cadger	.10	.85
Lilac, (Umbellata Lilacina)	Cadiz	.10	1.00

CANDYTUFT

CANNA Vaughan's Giant Flowered Mixture

CANDYTUFT—Continued.

	TEL. CIPHER.	OZ.	LB.
Carmine, (Umbellata Carminea)	Cadmia	$0.20	$2.00
Queen of Italy, pink dwarf true	Codong	.25	2.80
Snowflake, very dwarf, white	Cadre	.15	1.80
Dwarf Hybrids, mixed	Caffa	.30	3.00
All Colors Mixed 10 lbs., $5.00; 5 lbs. $2.60	Caftan	.10	.55
Coronaria "Princeps" (Little Prince)	Cagebird	.25	2.50
Sempervirens, white, perennial	Cail	2.00	
Gibraltarica, lilac, perennial	Cain	1.40	
Canna, **Crozy's**, best mixed 5 lbs., $5.00	Cakus	.10	1.10
Red Leaved Varieties	Calcutta	.15	1.60
Crozy's, Vaughan's Special Mixture, saved from our own collection of best 50 kinds	Cajoling	.25	2.80

CARNATION.

We call special attention to our Carnation Seed, which is raised by specialists.

Vienna Dwarf, extra choice mixed	Calf	$0.80	$10.00
Guillaud or Riveria Market, mx **1-16 oz., $2.00**	Calgar		
Double Perpet'l (Chabaud), mxd. ¼ oz., 50c.	Calico	1.50	
Marie Chabaud, yellow...1,000 seeds, $2.00	Califata		
Glowing Coal, brilliant red.1,000 seeds, $2.00	Caliga		
Fine Double Mixed	Calk	.75	10.00
Extra Choice Mixed	Calker	1.50	
Grenadin, double red, half high type	Camel	1.25	18.00
Grenadin, double white	Cameo	2.00	
Giant Flowered Malmaison	**Camelion**	.65	8.00
Giant of Nice, extra choice strain. new mixed, 1-32 oz., $1.50	**Camba**		

CARNATION Vaughan's Special Mixture

CELOSIA Thompsoni Magnifica

CARNATIONS—Continued.

	TEL. CIPHER.	OZ.	LB.
American Hybrids in finest mixture, 1,000 seeds $4.50	Calnay		
Improved Dwarf Margaret, mx	Calm	$1.00	$14.00
Margaret, white ⅛ oz., 15c	Calyx	.75	
" pink ⅛ oz., 15c	Calyxius	.75	
" crimson ⅛ oz., 25c	Callant	1.60	
" striped ⅛ oz., 15c	Caller	.75	
" yellow ¼ oz., 40c	Callosity	1.50	
" mixed	Callous	.50	6.00
Giant Margaret, white	Camber	2.00	
Giant Margaret, mixed	Cambric	2.00	
Vaughan's Special Mixture ⅛ oz., $3.00	Camelot		
Cardiospermum, see Balloon Vine.			
Castor Oil Bean, see Ricinus.			
Catananche Coerulea, blue	Catalonia	.35	
Coerulea Alba, white	Catarrh	.30	
Catchfly, See Silene Armeria.			

CELOSIA.

	TEL. CIPHER.	OZ.	LB.
Cristata, (Coxcomb) Tall sorts mixed	Camera	.15	1.85
Cristata Nana, **Dwarf** sorts mixed, ex. choice	Camés	1.25	16.00
" " **Dwarf** sorts good mixed	Camomial	.50	5.50
" " **President Thiers.** true	Camp	1.00	14.00
" " **Empress,** extra choice dwarf, crimson combs	Campaign	1.85	
" " Aurea, dwf., gldn. yellow cmbs	Campana	1.20	
" " Rosea, dwf., rose-cld. combs	Campaned	1.20	
" " Fire King, new ⅛ oz., 45c	Campanga	3.00	

CENTAUREA CYANUS—Vaughan's Special Mixture

CENTAUREA Imperialis White

CELOSIA—Continued.

	TEL. CIPHER.	OZ.	LB.
Plumosa, Triumph of the Exposition	Camper	$0.15	$1.35
" Mixed, feathered varieties	Can	.10	1.00
" Pride of Castle Gould.. 1/8 oz., 75c.	Canal	5.00	
" **Thompsoni Magnifica**, this is one of the best novelties, makes fine pot plants	Canalar	.40	4.50
" Ostrich Plume, crimson	Canary	.65	8.00
" Ostrich Plume, orange	Cancel	.65	8.00
Spicata	Carol	.20	

CENTAUREA.

Imperialis, Alba, pure white	Centaur	.30	3.50
Splendens, Purplish lilac	Centimp	.45	
Lilacina, Lilac	Centors	.45	
Favorita, Rosy lilac	Centurg	.45	
Mixed colors	Cental	.25	2.80
Gymnocarpa	Cease	.25	2.50
Candidissima (Dusty Miller)	Cebell	.80	10.00
Clementei	Centux	.40	
Cyanus (Corn Flower), Emperor William, blue	Cebus	.10	.85
" Fl. pl. mixed, semi-double, comes about 60 per cent true	Cedar	.15	1.50
" Bachelor's Button, mix. 10 lbs., $5.00	Cede	.10	.60
" Bachelor's Button, pink	Cebid	.10	1.20
" Double pure white	Cedula	.45	5.00
" Double blue	Ceduos	.45	5.00
" Double Lawson Pink	Cedilla	.45	5.00
" Dwarf Victoria, blue	Ceiled	.25	

CENTAUREA—Continued.

	TEL. CIPHER.	OZ.	LB.
Margaret, white	Celeste	$0.25	$2.80
Moschata, mixed, Sweet Sultan	Cellar	.10	1.20
Suaveolens, Yellow Sweet Sultan	Cement	.25	2.80
Americana, purple	Censer	.30	3.50
" Alba	Centalba	1.00	
Vaughan's Special Mixture includes all of the above	Centussis	.30	3.50
Centrosema Grandiflora	Cenure	.80	
Cerastium Tomentosum ⅛ oz., 65c.	Cerata		
Chelone Barbata Hybrida, mixed	Chaco	.25	
Barbata Torreyi	Chabbery	.15	
Lyonii	Chab	.70	
Cheiranthus Maritimus, see **Virginia** Stocks.			

CHRYSANTHEMUM.

	TEL. CIPHER.	OZ.	LB.
Coronarium, double white	Chat	$0.10	$0.90
" double golden yellow	Chaw	.10	.90
" double sulphur yellow	Check	.10	1.00
" double mixed 5 lbs., $3.25	Ched	.10	.70
" Pumilum Luteum Pl., Golden Ball	Century	.60	
Dunnetti Album pl., double white	Cheer	.25	
" **Aureum pl.**, double yellow	Cheesy	.25	
Carinatum, Eclipse (Chameleon)	Chemist	.10	1.40
" Golden Feather	Cher	.15	
" Single Mixed 5 lbs., $4.00	Cheroot	.10	.85
" The Sultan	Chelo	.15	
Inodorum Plenissimum, double white	Cherub	.30	3.50
" " Bridal Robe	Cherubic	1.00	
Segetum "Gloria" Morning Star	Cherubin	.10	1.00
Segetum "Helios," Evening Star	Chervice	.10	1.00
Double and Single Mixed, ann. sorts, 5 lbs, $4.50	Chess	.10	1.00
Frutescens, Paris Daisy	Chestnut	.30	3.50
Maximum, Ox-Eye-Daisy	Cheval	.25	2.50
Leucanthemum, Spring Marguerite	Chevalty	.25	2.50
Chinese and Japanese Vars., mixed, ⅛ oz., 45c.	Chide	3.25	
Japanese, Early Flowering Single, mixed, new, ⅛ oz., $1.00	Chief		
Uliginosum	Pyroe	1.00	

CINERARIA HYBRIDA.

	TEL. CIPHER.	OZ.	LB.
Large Flowering (Maxima) choicest mixture. 1-32 oz., $1.25; ⅛ oz., $4.00	Cinder		
Grandiflora, large-flowered, prize varieties, splendid mixed, 1-32 oz., $2.25	Cindery		
Vaughan's Columbian Mixture, 1-32 oz., $2.50	Cinderella		
Maxima Nana, extra choice mixed, dwarf, 1-16 oz $2.25	Cinlid		
	Cinkefoil		
Grandiflora, "Stella," 1-32 oz., $1.75	Cinnamole		
Large Flowering, sky-blue, 1-32 oz., 75c.	Cinnamate		
" " crimson, 1-32 oz., $1.00	Cinnamic		
" " old rose, 1-32 oz., $3.00	Cinnabar		
" " white, 1-32 oz., $1.00	Cinque	4.00	
Ordinary Mixed, ⅛ oz., 60c.	Cipher		
Double, best mixed, 1-32 oz., $1.00	Ciphering		
Radiata (Polyantha, Stellata) 1-16 oz., $1.50	Circle	.15	1.50
Cineraria Maritima Candidissima	Circline	$0.30	
" " " Diamond			

	TEL. CIPHER.	OZ.	LB.
Clarkia, Pulchella, Single mixed	Clam	.10	$0.80
Elegans fl. pl., double mixed	Clamber	20	2.40
Clematis Paniculata	Clasp	.35	3.50
Large Flowering, Jackmani Hybrids, mixed	Clear	1.25	
Cleome Pungens, Giant Spider Plant, true	Clease	.15	1.80
Clianthus Dampieri, Glory Pea of Australia	Cleff	1.25	
Cobaea Scandens, purple	Coax	.25	2.50
Scandens Flore Albo, white	Cobalt	.50	6.00
" mixed	Cobas	.40	4.00
Coccinea Indica, fine climber	Cocoloba	.60	
Cockscomb, see Celosia cristata.			
Coix **Lachrymae,** Job's Tears for sowing 10 lbs., $3.00	Cocoat	.05	.35
Coleus, Vaughan's Rainbow Mixt., 1-16 oz., $1.00.	Cobby	12.00	
Fine Mixed	Cobra	1.25	16.00
Extra Choice, large leaved, mix. ⅛ oz. $1.20	Cobweb	8.00	
" " " " copper-color 1-16 oz. $1.25	Cocaine		
Laciniated and Fringed 1-16 oz., $1.00	Cocoa		
Cordyline, see Dracaena.			
Collinsia, mixed 5 lbs., $1.75	Cockade	.10	.40
Columbine, see Aquilegia.			
Commelina Sellowiana ¼ oz., 35c	Cockent	1.25	
Convolvulus Major (Morning Glory), white	Cocoon	.10	.50
" " " " blue	Coda	.10	.50
" " " " crimson	Codex	.10	.50
" " " " striped	Codger	.10	.50
" " " " all colors mixed ......100 lbs., $27.00; 10 lbs., $3.00	Coerce	.10	.35
Imported Collection of 8 varieties, ea., 18c net.	Coercing		
Major, double mixed	Coercible	.15	1.70
Imperial Japanese, mixed 5 lbs., $3.50	Coffer	.10	.75
" " fancy fringed, best, 5 lbs., $7.00	Cofringed	.15	1.50
Minor, Dwarf Glory, mixed 5 lbs., $1.60	Cognate	.05	.35
Mauritanicus, for hanging baskets	Cognize	.30	
Coreopsis Lanceolata, golden yellow	Caboche	.20	2.00
Grandiflora, large flowering, golden yellow	Codak	.20	2.40
Cosmos, Giant-flowered, choice mixed	Cohorting	.10	1.10
Giant-Flowered, white	Coiled	.15	1.50
" " pink	Coins	.15	1.50
" " crimson	Code	.10	1.30
" " **Lady Lenox**	Coddin	.15	1.50
" " striped	Coddy	.35	4.00
Early Flowering Hybrids, mixed	Collapse	.20	2.00
" " Dawn, white	Collar	.20	2.40
" " **White,**	Collateral		
" " **Pink,**	Collation	.30	3.00
" " **Crimson**	Colleague	.20	2.40
Klondyke, yellow	Collect	.45	5.00
Marguerite	College	.25	2.80
Cowslip (Primula Veris)	Collate	1.00	
Cuphea Purpurea	Cupric	.25	
Platycentra ⅛ oz., 50c	Curate	3.50	

CYCLAMEN

DAHLIA—Vaughan's Special Mixture

CYCLAMEN PERSICUM.

		Tel. Cipher.	Oz.	Lb.
Fine Mixed	⅛ oz., 25c.	Cyanose	$1.50	
Giganteum, pure white, 1,000 seeds, $3.50;	per ⅛ oz., $1.00	Cyclide	...	
" Rose Marienthal, 1,000 seeds, $3.50;	per ⅛ oz., $1.00	Cyclone	..	
" Dark Crimson, 1,000 seeds, $3.50;	⅛ oz., $1.00	Cyclops	...	
" White with Carmine Eye, 1,000 seeds, $3.00;	per ⅛ oz., $1.00	Cygnet	...	
" Dark Rose. 1,000 seeds, $3.50;	⅛ oz., $1.00	Cygnus	...	
" Mixed. 1,000 seeds, $1.50, ⅛ oz., 60c.	1,000 seeds	Cycle	4.00	
Orchid-Flowered, mixed	$4.50	Cygnopsis		...
" " Pure White, 100 seeds, 65c	$5.00	Cylichna		...
" " Red, 100 seeds, 65c.	5.00	Cylichoton		...
" " White with eye, 100 seeds, 65c	$5.00	Cyltchoza		...
" " Pink, 100 seeds, 65c	5.00	Cylindrella		...
" " Lilac-Color, 100 seeds, 65c	$5.00	Cylindrical		...

NEW ENGLISH-GROWN CYCLAMEN.

	Tel. Cipher.		Tel. Cipher.
Rosy Morn	Czar.	Grandiflorum Album	Czyastio.
Picturatum	Czarina.	Princess of Wales	Czasth.
Excelsior	Czast	Mauve Queen	Czatab.
Princess May	Czaster.	Duke of Connaught	Czateg.
Salmon Queen	Czyasting.	Duke of Fife	Czateger.

Any of the above, per 1,000 seeds, $7.00; per 100 seeds, 90c.

Glory of Wandsbek, per 1,000 seeds $8.00 100 seeds $1.00 Cyat

	TEL. CIPHER.	OZ.	LB.
Cynoglossum Linifolium	Cylas	$0.10	$0.40
Cyperus Alternifolius, Umbrella Plant	Cylinder	.80	
Cypress Vine, White	Cymbal	.10	1.40
" " Scarlet	Cyprine	.10	1.40
" " Ivy-Leaved	Cypress	.15	1.80
" " Mixed	Cyprus	.10	1.30
Cardinal Climber pkt. (20 seeds) 12 cts. net			
Double Peony **Flowered Mixed**	Daelay	1.00	
Dahlia, Double mixed, good quality	Dace	.45	5.00
" " extra choice mixed	Dactyl	1.00	12.00
" " Cactus-Flowered, mixed	Daftness	.85	10.00
" " Cactus-Flowered, extra choice mixed	Dague	3.50	
" " Liliput, mixed	Dail	1.00	
" **Single Giant** Perfection, mixed	Dalmio	.15	1.8
" " Striped and Spotted	Dalle	.20	2.20
" " Mixed	Damas	.10	1.00
" " Collarette	Damper	1.00	
" " Zimpani (Black Cosmos)	Dabble	.45	
" " 20th Century	Daze	1.50	
" **Colossal,** new semi-double "Peony-flowered," mixed	Dazzle	.75	
" Vaughan's **Special Mixture,** dbl. and sgl.	Dame	3.50	
Daisy, see Bellis, Agathea, Brachycome and Chrysanthemum Maximum.			
Shasta Daisy, Alaska, best white	Dampare	1.00	14.00
Datura Fastuosa fl. pl., double mixed	Danaid	.15	1.60
Double White	Dancer	.15	1.80
Cornucopia	Dandy	.20	2.00
Triple-Flowered yellow (Golden Queen)	Darion	.20	2.00
Delphinium Formosum, blue	Deacon	.50	5.50
Formosum Coelestinum, (Pillar of Beauty)	Deadly	.55	6.00
Nudicaule, red ⅛ oz., 40c.	Deafen	2.80	
Elatum Hybridum, extra choice mixed	Dearth	.15	1.80
" " double hybrids, fine mixed	Deball	1.00	14.00
Kelway's Hybrids, an extra choice strain	Debar	4.00	
Zalil, yellow, splendid cut flower, ⅛ oz., 50c.	Debet	3.50	
Belladonna Hybrids	Debonair	2.50	
Chinese double **and** single, mixed	Deflect	.20	2.20
" **Album Grandiflorum,** white, fine cut-flower	Deflective	.25	2.80
" **Azureum,** blue	Deflector	.25	2.80
Cashmerianum, dark blue; fine.. ¼ oz., 75c.	Deflexion		
Caucasicum, sky-blue	Deflorate	.30	
Speciosum Glabratum, blue	Defluency	.40	
Sibiricum hybridum, blue shades	Degenerate	.40	
" Premium hybrids	Degenery	.80	
Vaughan's Special **Mixture** of **Perennial Varieties**	Defoliate	3.00	
See also Larkspur.			

DIANTHUS-PINKS.

Double Chinese Pink, choice mixed, 5 lbs., $8.50	Digest	.15	1.80
Single Chinese, extra choice mixed	Diminish	.15	1.80
Heddewigi fl. pl., double Japan, best mixed	Dimity	.45	5.00
Single, extra fine mixed	Dimly	.30	3.00
Eastern Queen	Dimness	.25	2.50
Crimson Belle	Dimple	.30	3.00
Snow Queen, best double white	Dinde	.90	12.00
Mourning Cloak, double	Diner	.60	7.00
Diadematus fl. pl., (Diadem Pink) double	Dingy	.45	5.00

DIANTHUS—Continued.

	TEL. CIPHER.	OZ.	LB.
Laciniatus fl. pl., Double fringed, mixed	Dining	$0.50	$6.00
" Lucifer fl. pl	Dinopisky	1.50	
" **Single fringed, mixed**	Dinsome	.25	2.60
" **Vesuvius,** orange scarlet	Dingle	.35	
" **Mephisto,** flaked and striped	Dintatler	.50	6.00
" **Mirabilis,** very fine	Dinsure	.40	4.50
" Mirabilis fl. pl. dbl. mxd	Disartge	.70	
" Albus Pl., "Snowdrift"	Dinopis	1.60	
Midnight, double blood-red	Diobol	.65	8.00
The Bride, single white	Diorite	.30	3.00
Double Striped	Diplaz	.75	
Count Kerchove	Dinopiste	.70	
Snowball, dwarf	Dipopa	.50	7.00
Fireball, dwarf	Dipper	.90	12.00
Marginatus, silver-edged, new	Diplomate	.50	6.00
Superbissima Mixed	Displaxy	.45	5.00
Double **Imperial Pinks,** (Imperialis fl. pl.) mixed	Disable	.20	2.20
New Princess Pink, very fine	Disabuse	.40	
Hybridus Latifolius Atrococcineus pl	Dirge	.50	6.00
Vaughan's Special Mixed, Dbl. and Single Pinks	Disarm	.50	6.00
Vaughan's Special Mixture, Single Pinks	Disband	.40	4.50
Vaughan's Special Mixture, Double Pinks	Disbar	.50	6.00
Plumarius, Single Pheasant's Eye Pink	Discard	.20	2.20
" New Early Flowering, double	Discount	2.50	
" Fl. Pl., double mixed	Disclose	.75	9.00
" **"Cyclops"**	Discurb	.85	12.00
" Semperflorens, double and single mxd	Disc	.50	6.00
" Diadematus	Discomb	1.00	
" Vaughan's Special mix	Discombed	1.25	
Barbatus, see Sweet William.			

	TEL. CIPHER.	OZ.	LB.
Dictamnus Fraxinella, Gas Plant	Distrain	$0.15	$1.80
" " Alba	Dack	.20	2.00
Digitalis (Foxglove) Purpurea Monstrosa, mixed	Dissintory	.30	3.50
" Purpurea, mixed	Dissent	.15	1.40
Gloxiniaeflora, mixed	Dissenter	.20	2.00
" Alba, white	Dissentment	.25	2.40
" Purple	Distant	.25	2.40
" Rose	Distaste	.25	2.40
Grandiflora yellow	Dissocial	.10	1.00
Maculata Iveryana, spotted varieties	Dissuade	.25	2.80
Vaughan's Special Mixture	Distent	.50	
Dimorphotheca Aurantiaca, Orange Daisy	Dividend	.60	6.50
" new Hybrids	Divider	1.20	
Dolichos (Hyacinth Bean), mixed, 5 lbs., $1.75	Doctor	.10	.40
Princess Helen (Daylight)	Doctrine	.10	.60
Purple Soudan	Dolent	.10	.60
Bush	Defend	.15	1.80
Dracaena Indivisa Lineata	Draggle	.30	
Indivisa	Drain	.20	2.00
Indivisa Latifolia	Draisine	.40	
Australis	Draper	.30	
Echeveria (Hen and Chicken), mxd 1,000 sds 65c.	Echas		
Metallica, 100 seeds, 25c; 1,000 seeds, $1.75	Elatior		
Secunda Glauca, 100 seeds for 15c, 1000 seeds, 65c	Elasticus		
Desmetiana. 80c per 1,000 seeds	Elate		
Echinacea Hybrida, beautiful new varieties	Echate	1.50	
Echinocystis Lobata, see Wild Cucumber.			
Echinops Ritro, blue, for bees	Echinops	.15	1.80

	TEL. CIPHER.	OZ.	LB.
Echinops, Sphaerocephalus	Echo	$0.20	
Edelweiss ....per ¼ oz., 45c..	Edenic ...	1.60	
Erigeron Aurantiacus Hybridus.....⅛ oz., 60c..	Enigma ...	4.00	
Grandiflorus Elatior...........¼ oz., 25c..	Enormous .	.80	
Eryngium Planum, dark blue..................	Era.......	.15	$1.50
" Amethystinum	Election ..	2.00	
" Alpinum	Equeal ...	1.20	
Erythrina Crista Galli, Coral Tree.............	Erupt	.40	4.50
Escholtzia, California Poppy, **Mandarin**..........	Eruption ..	.15	1.60
Californica, pure yellow ......5 lbs., $3.50..	Eregsiple ..	.10	1.25
" Mikado	Esoteric ..	.75	
" Rose Cardinal	Espace ..	.15	1.80
" **Rosy Morn**, Canaliculata Rosea........	Essay	.25	2.80
" **Glory of the West, or the Golden West**	Espoir ...	.15	1.50
" "Carmine King"	Espalier ..	.25	2.80
Maritima, Maltese Cross	Espohr ...	.15	1.40
Thorburni	Essence ..	.80	
Burbank's white crimson and gold.........	Essayist ..	.30	
Hunnemannia, Bush Escholtzia............	Hurdle ...	.25	3.00
Erecta Compacta Dainty Queen...........	Esculent .	1.00	
Mixed, many colors...........5 lbs., $3.25..	Estate	.10	.70
"Vaughan's Special" **Mixture**	Esteem ...	.30	3.50
Double White	Esther ...	.15	
" Pink	Esthetic ..	.20	
" Yellow	Estime ...	.15	
" Mixed	Estival ...	.20	
Eucalyptus Globulus, Blue Gum...............	Evylin ...	.35	
Eupatorium Fraseri	Estoc	.35	
Ageratoides	Estod	.25	2.80
Euphorbia Heterophylla, Mexican Fire Plant.....	Euphema .	.25	3.00
Variegata Snow-on-the-Mountain	Eva	.10	1.20
Everlasting Flowers, see Ammobium, Helichrysum Acroclineum, Rhodanthe, Xeranthemum and Gomphrena			
Feverfew, see Matricaria and Pyrethrum.			
Forget-Me-Not, see Myosotis			
Four O'Clock, see Marvel of Peru.			
Foxglove, see Digitalis.			
Freesia Refracta Alba........................	Freesia ...	.15	$1.40
" Hybrids ....1,000 seeds, $6.00..	Freezer ...		
Fuchsia, Dbl. and single mxd, 1,000 seeds, $2.35..	Fuchs		
" Double mixed ......1,000 seeds, $2.50..	Fugitive ..		
" Single mixed.......1,000 seeds, $2.25..	Fugacious .		
" Procumbens ....1,000 seeds $1.20..	Flight		
Gaillardia Lorenziana, double mixed............	Gainer ...	.15	1.50
Picta, mixed	Gainley ...	.10	.70
Grandiflora, perennial varieties, choice mixed.	Gainsaier .	.15	1.50
" Campacta, dwarf sorts..........	Gainsay ..	.25	3.00
" **Kelway's Newest Hybrids**.......	Galantous .	5.00	
" Maxima Kermesina Splendens...	Galantery	.50	
" Sulphurea Oculata	Gala	.40	
" Semipiena	Gem	.85	
Gaura Lindheimeri, white, very fine............	Gesulate .	.15	
Gazania, Hybrids, mixed........100 seeds, 60c..	Gild		
Gentiana Acaulis, dark blue, fine..............	General ..	.60	
Geranium, Apple-scented 100 seeds 40cts 1,000 seeds ....$3.00..	Generosity.		
Zonale Single, fine mixed.	Generous .	.75	10.00
Zonale Single, extra, large-flowering, mixed..	Genepa ...	1.50	
Lady Washington, 1,000 seeds, $8.00 100, $1.00	Generu ..		

	TEL. CIPHER.	OZ.	LB.
Gerbera Jamesoni Hybrids 65c per 100 seeds; $5.00 per 1,000 seeds	Genial		
Geum Atrosanguineum pl., semi-double, red	Genesis	$0.60	
Heldreichi large orange flowers	Gold	1.00	
Gilia, mixed ... 5 lbs., $1.35	Gilding	.10	$0.30
Gilly Flower, see Stocks.			
Gladiolus Praecox, annual gladiolus	Glade	1.50	
Glaucium Luteum (Horn Poppy)	Gladden	.10	1.00
Globe Amaranth (Gomphrena) mixed	Gloher	10	.65
" " White	Gloom	.10	.90
" " Red	Gloomier	.10	.90
Gloxinia Hybrida Grandiflora, best strains in finest mixture ... 1-32 oz., $1.25	Glossom		
Fine mixed ... 1-32 oz., 75c	Glosam		
Godetia, many sorts mixed ... 5 lbs., $5.50	Gloot	.10	1.20
New Dwarf Hybrids, mixed	Goblet	.15	1.80
Duchess of Albany	Goblin	.20	
Gloriosa	Goddess	.30	
Rosamunde	Godless	.30	
Lady Satin Rose	Godly	.30	
The Bride	Goggles	.15	
Golden Rod	Goose	.10	1.20
Gomphrena, see Globe Amaranth.			
Gourds, Dish-Cloth	Gorge	.10	.90
Dipper, or Siphon	Gorgon	.10	1.00
Japanese Nest Egg	Goring	.10	1.00
Japanese Bottle	Gossamer	.20	2.00
Sugar Trough	Gosling	.10	.90
Ornamental Pomegranate	Gospel	.10	1.20
Hercules Club	Gossip	.10	1.20
Bottle, large	Gotham	.10	1.20
Calabash, Pipe Gourd	Gothic	.15	1.80
Turk's Turban	Gouge	.15	1.60
Mock Orange	Gourder	.10	1.00
Apple-shaped	Gouty	.10	1.00
Pear-shaped	Govan	.10	1.00
Spoon	Gaudy	.15	
Many sorts, mixed ... 5 lbs., $5.50	Govern	.10	1.00
Small sorts, mixed	Grabat	.10	1.00
Gourds, Imported Collection of 6 var., ea. 12c.	Grabble		
" " " 12 var., ea. 25c.	Graceful		
Grasses, Ornamental Varieties, mixed	Grace	.10	.70
Grevillea Robusta	Grebe	.40	4.00
Gypsophila Paniculata, fine perennial	Gypsum	.20	2.20
Paniculata fl. pl. ... 1-16 oz., $1.00	Gypsy		
Acutifolia	Gyral	.10	
Muralis, pink, perennial	Gypter	.25	2.40
Elegans, white (Angel's Breath) 10 lbs., $3.00	Gyrate	.10	.35
" Rosea ... 5 lbs., $1.50	Gyves	.10	.35
" Alba Grandiflora	Gyzat	.10	.60
" Carminea new	Gyral	.35	3.00
Helenium Autumnale Superbum, tall golden yellow	Heat	1.20	
Bigelowi, yellow, for cutting	Hearken	2.25	
Hoopesi, yellow	Herbal	.30	
Riverton Beauty	Heating		
Riverton Gem	Heather		
Helianthus, see Sunflower.			
Helichrysum Monstrosum fl. pl., double mixed	Healer	.25	2.50
Heliopsis Pitcheriana, golden yellow, early	Height	.20	
Helipterum Sandfordi	Held	.25	
Heliotrope, fine mixed ... ¼ oz., 15c	Hearty	.50	6.50
Mammoth Flowered, mixed	Helicon	.80	11.00

	TEL. CIPHER.	OZ.	LB.
Hesperis Matronalis (Sweet Rocket)	Helmet	$0.15	$1.50
Matronalis Alba, white	Hermit	.15	1.50
Heuchera Sanguinea ... ¼ oz., 35c.	Hewer	1.20	
Sanguineus Splendens	Hexagon	1.50	
Brizoiodes	Hexagonal	1.50	
Hibiscus, Giant Yellow or Sunset (Golden Bowl)	Hiatus	.50	5.00
Crimson Eye	Hidden	.15	1.80
Moscheutos, roseus	Hideous	.20	2.40
Mallow Marvels, new	Hierarch	.50	5.00
Hollyhock, Double White	Hoery	.85	12.00
" " Pink	Hoarse	.65	7.00
" " Deep Rose	Hockey	.65	7.00
" " Crimson	Hodman	.60	6.50
" " Blood-Red	Hoeve	.75	10.00
" " Dr. Faust, black	Homan	.60	6.50
" " Yellow	Hoist	.65	7.00
" " Salmon	Homer	.85	12.00
" **Mixed, extra** choice (Chaters)	Homily	.75	10.00
" " Mixed, very good quality	Honesty	.35	4.00
" Single mixed	Hoodwink	.25	2.50
" **Mammoth Allegheny, best mixed**	Hoof	.50	6.00
" Everblooming, single mixed	Hoofing	.25	2.80
" " **Double Annual, mixed**	Hope	.35	4.00
Humulus Japonicus, Japanese Hop	Hook	.15	1.60
Japonicus fol. var., variegated	Hoop	.15	1.80
Hunnemannia Fumariaefolia, Bush Escholtzia	Hurdle	.25	3.00
Hyacinth Bean, see Dolichos.			
Hyacinthus Candicans	Hurra	.10	
Iberis, see Candytuft.			
Ice Plant (Mesembryanthemum Crystallinum)	Iceland	.10	1.00
Impatiens Sultani, brill't carmine, 1-16 oz., 75c.	Image	8.00	
Holsti, new, very fine ... 1-16 oz., 85c.	Imitate		
" New hybrids ... 1-16 oz., 40c.	Imitator		
Incarvillea Delavayi ... ⅛ oz., 25c.	Incar	1.20	
Grandiflora	Imagery	1.80	
Inula Ensifolia, golden yellow, dwarf	Idol	.60	
" Glandulosa Grandiflora ... ⅛ oz., $1.00	Idler		
Ionopsidium Acaule, Diamond Flower	Iono	.50	
Ipomoea Noctiflora, Moonflower, white seeded	Ipecac	.30	3.00
" " black seeded	Ipfam	.20	2.20
Hybrid, **Moonflower**, early blooming	Iphisa	.30	3.00
Giant Pink (Northern Light)	Ipjar	.20	2.40
Leari, dark blue, splendid	Ipocras	1.00	14.00
Bona Nox, large blue flowers	Ireful	.10	.60
Setosa, Brazilian Morning Glory	Irene	.25	2.80
Rubra-cœrulea, or "Heavenly-Blue	Iridal	.30	3.20
Early Flowering, new	Irish	1.00	
Imperialis, Japanese Morning Glory ... 5 lbs., $3.50	Coffer	.10	.75
Imperialis, Japanese fancy fringed, extra ... 5 lbs., $7.00	Cofringed	.15	1.50
Rochester Morning Glory	Cofroit	.15	1.80
Coccinea, scarlet, very free	Incident	.10	.70
Sanguinea	Miton	.10	1.00
Iris Kaempferi	Iris	.35	3.80

	TEL. CIPHER.	OZ.	LB.
Jacobaea Elegans fl. pl., double mixed	Jewel	$0.35	$4.00
Job's Tears, see Coix Lachrymae			
Kenilworth Ivy, Linaria Cymbalaria, pink	Lien	.90	
Cymbalaria Alba, white	Lievre	.80	
Kochia Tricophylla, the true Summer Cypress ... 5 lbs., $3.20	Kochia	.10	.70
Kudzu Vine, Pueraria Thunbergiana	Kudzu	.40	4.50
Lantana Hybrida, mixed	Ladle	.10	1.20
Bruant's Dwarf Hybrids, mixed	Laflin	.20	2.00
Larkspur, Emperor, extra choice mixed	Laggard	.10	1.20
Double Dwarf Rocket, best mixed	Lambeau	.10	1.00
Double Tall Rocket, best mixed	Lambkin	.10	1.20
Newport Pink	Lamed	.50	
Double Giant Hyacinth-Flowered, mixed	Lambrock	.15	1.40
See also Delphinium.			
Lathyrus Latifolius (Everlasting Pea), mixed	Lament	.15	1.80
Latifolius Albus, white	Lampion	.20	2.50
" Red	Languid	.15	1.60
" **Pink Beauty,** very fine	Lanora	.15	1.60
" White Pearl, new	Lank	2.00	
Lavatera Arborea Variegata, leaves mottled with yellow	Lane	.30	
Lemon Verbena, Aloysia Citriodora	Leaden	1.20	16.00
Leontopodium, Edelweiss ... ¼ oz., 45c.	Edenic	1.60	
Liatris Elegans ... ¼ oz., 40c.	Leakage		
Spicata ... ¼ oz., 50c.	Leap		
Linaria Cymbalaria, Kenilworth Ivy	Lien	.90	
" " White	Lievre	.80	
Linum Grandiflorum Rubrum, Scarlet Flax, ... 5 lbs., $3.00	Lifeless	.10	.70
Perenne, Blue	Lifeline	.10	1.00
" White	Lifelong	.10	1.00
" Mixed	Light	.10	.90
Flavum, perennial, yellow, fine	Liege	.60	
Luteum, bright yellow, annual	Limb	.60	
Lobelia, Crystal Palace Compacta, true	Loading	1.00	14.00
Compacta Firmament, new	Local	1.80	
Speciosa, dark flowers and foliage, true	Loaf	.35	4.00
Erinus, Emperor William, dwf., choice strain	Loamy	.75	9.00
" Dwarf, White Lady	Lobesam	.45	5.00
" White	Lobster	.35	4.00
" Gracilis, blue	Lobule	.25	2.80
" Pumila Splendens (Bedding Queen)	Locate	.90	12.00
" Mixed	Locker	.25	2.80
Hamburgia, for hanging baskets, ⅛ oz. 40c.	Loan	2.50	
Cardinalis	Logical	1.75	
Syphilitica, blue ... ⅛ oz., 30c.	Loiner	2.00	
Lophospermum Scandens	Loosen	1.00	
Luffa Acutangula, Dish Rag Gourd	George	.10	.90
Lupinus, Annual sorts mixed, tall	Lunary	.10	.70
" Annual sorts mixed, dwarf	Luncheon	.15	1.20
Polyphyllus albus	Lunch	.15	1.60
" atrocoeruleus	Lung	.15	1.60
" roseus	Lunular	.60	
" mixed	Lunatic	.10	1.00
Arboreus Snow Queen	Lunater	.50	
Hybridus Roseus	Lunation	.15	1.80
Subcarnosus, blue, dwarf	Lurch	.25	

MARIGOLD—Double Tall African, Special Mixture

	TEL. CIPHER.	OZ.	LB.
Lychnis Alpina	Lobby	$2.00	
Chalcedonica, scarlet	Lynx	.15	$1.60
Chalcedonica Alba, white	Lunchy	.20	2.00
Haageana hybrida mixed, extra choice	Lyre	.70	9.00
Haageana, scarlet	Lyarting	1.00	
Haageana, hybrida nana, mixed	Lyartsam	.80	
Sieboldi, white, fine	Lyme	1.00	
Lythrum Roseum Superbum	Lythrum	.15	1.60

MARIGOLD.

	TEL. CIPHER.	OZ.	LB.
Marigold, Double Tall African mixed, 5 lbs., $7.00	Madame	.15	1.50
" Double Tall African, Orange King	Mackerel	.15	1.80
Eldorado, a fine strain	Mage	.15	1.80
Double Dwarf African, mixed, (Pride of the Garden)	Madcap	.20	2.00
Double Tall African, Lemon Queen	Madcaper	.15	1.80
Vaughan's Special Mixture, Tall sorts	Maderio	.25	2.80
Vaughan's Special Mixture, Dwarf sorts	Magasin	.25	2.80
Double Tall French, mixed	Mahdist	.15	1.50
Double Dwarf French, gold striped	Maimed	.15	1.80
" " " Aurora, new	Maddon	.25	2.80
Double Dwarf French, mixed, 5 lbs., $5.50	Malofic	.15	1.25
Legion of Honor	Maltese	.15	1.60
Silver King	Manage	.15	1.60
Golden Star, new	Manageable	1.00	
Golden Liliput, double	Madly	.20	2.00
Imported Collection French Marigold, 6 kinds, each, net, 15c	Maringo		
Imported Collection African Marigold, 6 kinds, each, net, 15c	Marigon		

See also Calendula.

MIGNONETTE Vaughan's Giant Machet

	TEL. CIPHER.	OZ.	LB.
Marvel of Peru, Four o'clock, mixed, 100 lbs., $30.00; 10 lbs., $3.25	Marel	$0.10	$0.35
Tom Thumb, dwarf, mixed	Margin	.10	.55
Variegated Leaved, mixed	Marine	.10	.45
Longiflora Alba, sweet scented	Marrow	.10	1.00
Mathiola Bicornis, Evening Scented Stock,	Mature	.10	.85
Matricaria Capensis fl. pl., double white Feverfew	Matron	$0.15	$1.60
Capensis Alba Plenissima	Max	.25	2.50
Eximia fl. pl., "Golden Ball" .... ¼ oz., 35c.	Martyr	1.20	
Maurandya, mixed	Maxim	.75	10.00
" Purpurea Grandiflora .... ⅛ oz., 25c.	Mausoleum		
" Barclayana Alba .... ⅛ oz., 25c.	Maw		
" Barclayana .... ⅛ oz., 20c.	Maul		
Melothria Punctata, splendid annual climber	Melo	.80	

MIGNONETTE.

Mignonette Grandiflora, large flowering, 100 lbs., $45.00; 10 lbs., $4.75	Microbe	.10	.50
Golden Queen	Midnight	.15	1.80
Golden Queen, American grown	Middle	.10	.80
Machet, American grown	Midway	.10	1.00
" Vaughan's Selected Stock	Might	.50	5.50
" Golden	Miglate	.35	4.00
" Golden, American grown	Middling	.10	1.00
" White Pearl .... ¼ oz., 25c.	Mignard	.85	

VAUGHAN'S NASTURTIUMS.

Mignonette—Continued

	TEL. CIPHER.	OZ.	LB.
Bismarck, an improved Machet	Mildew	$0.45	$5.00
Goliath, or Red Giant	Milward	1.00	12.00
Miles' Spiral	Milton	.10	1.40
Spiralis Defiance	Milthorp	.25	2.80
Gabriele, extra large and sweet, fine for cutting	Mimic	.25	2.80
New York Market, for greenhouse, ⅛ oz., 75c	Mineral	5.00	
Large Flowering Pyramidal	Mingle	.30	3.00
Giant White Spiral (Reseda Alba)	Miniate	.10	1.20
Many sorts mixed 5 lbs., $2.75; 10 lbs. $5.00	Minify	.10	.60
Mimosa Pudica. Sensitive Plant	Minstrel	.15	1.80
Mimulus Moschatus, Musk Plant	Miracle	.85	
Tigrinus, single mixed	Misded	.70	
Tigrinus fl. pl., Double Monkey Flower	Misery	1.20	
" New Large-Flowering, single (Queen's Prize)	Mister	1.20	
Mina Lobata	Mite	.50	6.00
Sanguinea, one of our best annual climbers	Miton	.10	
Mirabilis, see Marvel of Peru.			
Momordica Balsamina, see Balsam Apple.			
Monarda Didyma...100 seeds, 25c; 1,000, $1.50	Mist		
" Hybrida Mixed	Misuse	.50	
Moon Flower, see Ipomoea.			
Morning Glory, see Convolvulus and Ipomea.			
Musa Ensete, per 100 seeds, 65c; 1,000, $5.00	Musa		
Myosotis, Forget-Me-Not, Alpestris, blue	Myoid	.35	4.00
Alpestris, white	Myopia	.30	3.50
Indigo Blue, Vaughan's Royal	Myself	.50	5.00
Eliza Fanrobert	Myraid	.50	6.00
Victoria, Dwarf, sky-blue	Myrrh	.65	7.00
Hybrida. Ruth Fischer, new 1-32 oz., $1.50	Musical		
Star of Love...1-8 oz., 50c	Music	3.00	
Dissitiflora	Mythic	2.00	
Palustris Semperflorens	Mython	1.00	
Palustris	Mytil	1.40	
Oblongata, very fine, blue, blooms in 8 weeks	Mytle	.50	6.00
Mixed, many kinds	Mystery	.30	3.50

DWARF NASTURTIUMS.

	TEL. CIPHER.	¼ LB.	LB.	10 LBS
Aurora, chrome yellow, blotched crimson...	Naples	$0.15	$0.40	$3.50
Bronze	Nardoo ...	.15	.40	3.50
Beauty, scarlet, blotched canary..........	Narcoma ..	.15	.40	3.50
Chameleon, mixed, true French strain......	Nargil	.15	.45	4.25
Cloth of Gold, flowers scarlet, foliage yellow.	Narrate ...	.15	.50	4.75
Coccineum, dark scarlet..................	Narrow ...	.15	.40	3.50
Crystal Palace Gem, sulphur, spotted maroon......................	Narwhal ..	.15	.40	3.60
David Burpee, new wavy foliage, oz., 20c..	Narwold ..	.50	2.00	
Empress of India, deep crimson, dark leaved	Nascent ...	.15	.45	4.30
Golden King, rich golden color, true........	Nassau	.15	.45	4.20
King of Tom Thumbs, deep scarlet, dark-leaved......................	Nastus	.15	.40	3.80
King Theodore, rich red, dark bluish foliage.	Nasute	.15	.40	3.80
Ladybird, yellow, barred with crimson.....	Nasy	.15	.45	4.25
Pearl, whitish	Natal	.15	.40	3.80
Prince Henry, yellow, marbled with scarlet.	Nation	.15	.40	3.60
Queen of Tom Thumbs, crimson..........	Nationate .	.25	.90	
" " " " deep organe scarlet.	Nativity ...	.40	1.30	
" " " " mixed colors	National ..	.20	.85	
Regelianum, purplish violet..............	Native	15.	.40	3.65
Ruby King, a peculiar blue-tinted red, true.	Nature	15	.45	4.25
Spotted King. See Ladybird.				
Vesuvius, a rich salmon rose, very fine.....	Naun	.15	.45	4.20
Yellow, (Luteum)	Nautical ..	.15	.40	3.60
Dwarf Sorts, all colors mixed, 100 lbs. $22.00	Naval	.10	.30	2.50
Dark, leaved varieties, mixed............	Nautilus ...	.10	.35	3.25
Liliput, choice mixture of Dwarf Lobbs....	Navir	.15	.45	4.25
Snow Queen, pure white............	Nasqueen ..	.20	.75	

"VAUGHAN'S SPECIAL MIXTURE"—Navy

"Vaughan's Special Mixture" of Dwarf Nasturtiums will give a larger variety of colors in even proportions than any other Nasturtium mixture for it is put up by ourselves from named sorts, which have the richest and most varied combination of colors ever produced, showing odd colors hitherto unknown among flowers.

Per ¼ lb., 20c; lb., 65c; 10 lbs., $6.00; 100 lbs., $50.00.

TALL NASTURTIUMS.

We are headquarters on these and carry large stocks.

Lobb's, in sorts and mixed, see Tropæolum.	TEL. CIPHER.	¼ LB.	LB.	10 LBS.
Chameleon, extra choice mixture..........	Neburg	$0.15	$0.50	$4.75
Coccineum, bright scarlet.................	Necket	.10	.35	3.25
Coquette, similar to Chameleon............	Necktie ...	.15	.50	4.80
Dunnett's Orange (Sunlight), bright orange.	Necre	.10	.35	3.25
Edward Otto, brownish lilac...............	Nedir	.10	.35	3.35
Golden Cloth, scarlet flower, yellow foliage..	Negger ...	.10	.40	3.80
Heinemanni, chocolate color..............	Neled	.10	.35	3.25
Hemisphericum, orange, very handsome....	Neiler	.10	.40	3.70
Ivy Leaved Mixed.........................	Neilocan ...	.25	1.00	
Jupiter, California sort, yellow, large......	Neiling ...	.15	.45	4.20
King Theodore, rich, deep red, dark foliage.	Neinsook .	.15	.45	4.20
Luteum, yellow	Neire	.10	.35	3.30
Pearl, (Moonlight) whitish...............	Nemable ..	.15	.40	3.65
Prince Henry, light yellow, marbled scarlet.	Nemeless ..	.10	.35	3.30
Regelianum, rich crimson, one of the best..	Nemesake .	.10	.35	3.20
Scheuermani, straw color, spotted.........	Neming	.10	.35	3.20
" Coccineum, scarlet striped....	Nency	.10	.40	3.70

TALL NASTURTIUMS—Continued.

	TEL. CIPHER.	¼ LB.	OZ.	LB.
Shillingi, bright yellow, maroon blotches	Nendino	$0.10	$0.35	$3.20
Vesuvius, salmon rose, dark-leaved, extra	Nendus	.15	.40	3.80
Von Moltke, bluish rose	Nenism	.10	.40	3.70
Tall sorts in finest mixture, 100 lbs., $20.00	Netar	.10	.25	2.20
Madam Gunther's Hybrids, true. We have an extra choice strain	Neuf	.15	.40	3.75
Variegated leaved mixed	Nibated	.15	.60	5.50

"VAUGHAN'S SPECIAL" Mixture of Tall Nasturtium—Tel. Cipher "Nett." Includes the above sorts of Tall as well as the Lobb's Nasturtiums, the beautiful **Hybrids** of **Madam Gunther**, and the Canary Bird Creeper, and is the finest mixture ever offered. ¼ lb., 15c; lb., 50c; 10 lbs., $4.75; 100 lbs., $45.00.

	TEL. CIPHER.	OZ.	LB.
Nemophila, mixed ....10 lbs., $3.50	Nibula	$0.10	$0.40
Nicotiana Affinis, large, white, very fragrant	Nickel	.20	2.40
Affinis Hybrids	Nook	.25	2.75
Sylvestris, very beautiful, sweet, pure white	Niedlic	.10	1.50
Sanderae	Nicola	.25	2.80
" New **Hybrids**, mixed	Nibble	.20	2.80
Nierembergia Gracilis, light blue, dwarf	Nigard	.35	
Nigella, mixed ....10 lbs., $3.75	Nigella	.10	.40
Hispanica, blue	Nigelto	.10	1.00
" Alba, white	Nigasta	.10	1.00
Damascena, Miss Jekyll, double blue	Nigastow	.25	2.50
Nolana, mixed	Noose	10	.50
Nycterinia Capensis, white, very sweet. ⅛ oz., 10c.	Nyctea	.50	
Oenothera, Evening Primrose, mixed	Oenomel	.10	.60
Frazeri	Omnibus	2.00	
Macrocarpa	Omniscient	.40	
Taraxacifolia Alba	Onerary	.60	
Rosea, Mexican Primrose	Oertel	.40	
Youngi	Orology	1.00	
Ornamental Grasses, mixed	Ornate	.10	.70
Oxalis Tropæoloides, dark yellow flowers, brown foliage	Oxa	.60	
Rosea, very fine	Oxalite	1.75	
" Alba	Oyant	1.75	
Valdiviana, yellow, sweet	Ozone	.30	
Pandanus Utilis, 100 seeds, 80c; 1,000 seeds, $7.00.	Pantry		

PANSIES.

GIANT-FLOWERED SORTS.

We are having our Pansy seed grown by some of the best European Pansy specialists and are therefore in position to offer the best qualities at prices that are as low, and in many cases, lower than those of German wholesale seedsmen. We invite comparison:.

	TEL. CIPHER.	OZ.	LB.
Giant Adonis, light blue	Pacage	$1.00	$14.00
" **Andromeda**, rose with lavender ⅛ oz., 20c.	Pacer	1.25	
" **Atrosanguinea**, dark red	Pacha	1.00	
" **Aureola**, lower petals crimson, with dark blotches upper petals light yellow ...... ⅛ oz., 30c.	Pacific	2.00	
" **Auricula Flowered**, (Bronze) fine shades	Pacifier	.80	10.00

PANSIES—Giant Flowering Sorts—Continued.

	TEL. CIPHER.	OZ.	LB.
Giant **Aurora**, pure white	Pacte	$0.85	$10.00
" **Beaconsfield**, purple violet, top petals blue	Padous	.90	12.00
" Black (King of the Blacks)	Page	.85	10.00
" **Boulogne Giants**, extra...... ⅛ oz., $2.00	Pagjot	14.00	
" Bridesmaid, lovely apple-blossom	Paginer	1.35	20.00
" **Bugnot**, extra choice	Pagode	1.50	20.00
" " **Elite**, the best strain	Paien	3.00	
" **Butterfly Mixture**	Paix	.65	8.00
" Cardinal Brilliant red	Painting	1.50	
" Cassier, 3 and 5 blotched, extra	Paison	1.00	14.00
" " 5 blotched yellow (Pres. McKinley)	Paitre	1.80	24.00
" " 5 blotched white (Pres. Carnot)	Pair	1.25	16.00
" " Hortensia-red	Palable	1.25	16.00
" Comet	Pagomot	1.00	
" **Diana**, cream color	Pageant	.85	10.00
" Eros, velvety brown, edged golden yellow	Paging	1.00	14.00
" Emperor William, rich metallic blue	Palais	.90	12.00
" Emperor Francis Joseph	Palmistry	2.80	
" **Fiery Faces**, (Fire King), red with black blotches	Palefrois	1.25	16.00
" **Freya**, silver-edged purple	Paleron	1.00	14.00
" Golden Queen, pure yellow	Palet	.90	12.00
" Indigo King, indigo blue	Paletono	1.00	14.00
" **Mad. Perret**, lovely shades of rose and pink	Paleur	.85	10.00
" **Masterpiece**, new strain with fluted petals	Palir	1.50	22.00
" " originator's stock	Palisse	3.50	
" Mauve Queen delicate mauve, lower petals blotched carmine	Palissya	.75	10.00
" Orchid-Flowered, rose and light shades	Palister	1.00	14.00
" " " Superba	Palmated	1.80	
" " " Sunlight	Plametto	2.00	
" Daybreak	Palpably	1.80	
" " " Almond Blossom	Palpitate	1.80	
" " " Mammoth	Palsied	2.00	
" Peacock or Pheasant's Eye, superb	Palm	1.00	
" **Parisian Striped**, very striking	Palmier	.85	10.00
" **Paris Market**, a very fine mixture	Palatay	.75	10.00
" Pretiosa ground color rosy crimson, violet blotches white margin	Palmira	1.00	
" Prince Bismarck. light brown shades	Palot	.90	12.00
" **Prince Henry**, darkest blue	Palovate	1.00	14.00
" Purple, rich color	Palpa	.85	12.00
" Purple King	Palsy	1.20	
" **Psyche**, violet bordered white, ⅛ oz., 25c	Palus	1.75	
" Raphael blue veins and violet blotches on white ground	Palsied	2.00	
" Rosy Morn, purplish crimson with clear white edge	Paddle	2.00	
" Ruby-Red, rich shades of red	Pantheon	.85	10.00
" **Siegfried**, brown shades, white margined	Pantheist	1.50	
" **Striped**, a fine strain	Pamer	.85	10.00
" **Trimardeau**, mixed	Palmist	.65	8.00
" Victoria, wine red	Palpable	1.25	
" Violet Blue	Pampe	.90	12.00
" Vulcano dark red with fine large black blotches	Pampfly	1.50	20.00
" **White with large purple eye**	Pamphlet	**.85**	**10.00**
" **Yellow**, with large black eye	Panache	**.85**	**10.00**

VAUGHAN'S GIANT MIXTURE—Pancarte.

This mixture is specially made up by ourselves from all of the separate colors of the Giant Pansies and several special strains which cannot be had in any other way.

Price, per lb., $25.00; 1/4 lb., $6.50; oz., $2.00.

		oz.
Vaughan's Cut Flower Mixture	Pandect	$6.00

PANSY—Chicago Parks Bedding Varieties.

	TEL. CIPHER.	1/4 OZ.	OZ.	LB.
Atrosanguinea, dark blood-red	Panse	$0.15	$0.60	$7.00
Auricula Colors	Pansu	.15	.50	6.00
Azure-blue, velvety, dark	Panta	.15	.50	6.00
Black, with Gold Bronze	Panth	.15	.50	
Blue-Black	Pantin	.15	.60	
Cardinal, rich scarlet	Paon	.20	.75	10.00
Coquette de Poissy, slate or mouse color	Papa	.15	.60	7.00
Dr. Faust, or King of the Blacks	Papegal	.15	.55	6.50
Diana, cream color	Papeland	.15	.60	
Emperor Frederick	Papeterie	.15	.60	
Emperor William, ultra-marine blue, dark center	Papier	.15	.60	7.00
Fairy Queen, sky-blue, silver border	Papil	.15	.50	6.00
Fire King, red, yellow margin	Papilesse	.15	.55	6.50
Golden Gem, pure yellow	Papilo	.20	.65	8.00
Gold Margined	Papoose	.15	.50	6.00
Light Blue, delicate shade	Parade	.15	.55	6.50
Lord Beaconsfield purple violet	Paradox	.15	.55	6.50
Mahogany Colors	Paragon	.20	.65	8.00
Meteor	Paramo	.25	.65	8.00
Peacock, (Quadricolor Spectabilis), royal purple	Parboil	.15	.50	6.00
Pelargoniflora	Parbleu	.20	.65	7.00
Prince Bismarck, bronze and light brown	Parcel	.15	.50	6.00
Quadricolor (Pheasant's Eye), sky-blue, edged violet	Parch	.15	.50	6.00
Red Riding Hood	Pardon	.15	.55	6.50
Silveredge, dark, light edge	Paring	.15	.50	6.00
Snow Queen, pure white	Parish	.20	.60	6.50
Striped and Mottled, extra choice	Parity	.20	.60	7.00
Victoria, red	Parole	.20	.70	8.00
Wallflower Colors	Paromet	.20	.60	7.00
White, with black eye	Parquet	.15	.50	6.00
Yellow, with black eye	Parrat	.15	.50	5.50
Sweet-scented	Passage	.25	.90	10.00

CHICAGO PARKS BEDDING PANSIES—Panor.

"Choice Mixed." All the above	.45	5.00
Bugnot and Cassier types mixed	.85	10.00

IMPROVED GERMAN MIXTURE PANSIES.—Panne.

This is a mixture of three strains from different German Growers, and is made up mostly of separate colors, with sufficient percentage of white and yellow.............. 1.00 12.00

PANSY. Good Mixed. many colors.............Pansage, ..$0.30 3.50

VAUGHAN'S "UP-TO-DATE", INTERNATIONAL—Pallia

THE WORLD'S BEST PANSIES

Vaughan's International is, we firmly believe, the best **Pansy mixture in existence**, because it is composed of the cream of 10 Pansy Specialists' collections. It contains besides the fancy selections of these growers all the separate colors and strains in cultivation, carefully prepared by ourselves, so we **know just what it should produce.**

This is one of the specialties which has established the reputation of Vaughan's Seeds, and our customers can readily see why it is our most earnest endeavor to make Vaughan's International Pansy Mixture better than ever. **Per ⅛ oz., $1.00; oz., $7.00; lb., $90.00.**

	TEL. CIPHER.	OZ.	LB.
Papaver, see Poppy.			
Passiflora, Mammoth Passion-flower, blue	Passing	$0.65	$8.00
Incarnata	Passable	.60	
Gracilis	Passive	.40	
Pelargonium, see Geranium.			
Peltaria Alliacea	Passonist	1.20	
Pennisetum Ruppellianum, Purple Feather Grass	Passion	.20	2.00
Longistylum	Passionate	.15	1.80
Pentstemon, large-flowering hybrids, mixed	Peage	1.20	
Digitalis, white tinted violet	Peach	.20	
Pubescens	Peace	.20	
Pulchellus Hybridus	Peaceable	.45	
Very fine mixed	Peasant	.20	2.00
Pepper, Vaughan's Xmas (Chamaleon). ⅛ oz., 15c.	Pegasus	1.00	
Perilla Nankinensis	Perilla	.10	.50

PETUNIA HYBRIDA.

	TEL. CIPHER.	OZ.	LB.
Petunia Hybrida, fine mixed.....5 lbs., $11.00	Peerage	.25	2.40
Hybrida, finest mxd. (part from named sorts)	Peevish	.35	3.50
Alba, white	Pelagic	.30	
Carmen Sylva, (Baby Blue)	Pelf	.70	
Violet Blue	Pelican	2.00	
Blotched and Striped (Inimitable)	Pellet	.40	4.00
Snowball, Dwarf white	Penance	.85	10.00
General Dodds, blood-red	Penas	.30	
Countess of Ellesmere, pink with white throat	Pencast	.25	2.50
Venosa, light red, veined	Pencave	.35	
Howard's Star, fine	Pelt	.75	10.00
Hybrida Nana Compacta. Rosy Morn	Pelter	1.00	
" " " Gloria, pink	Peltinger	2.00	
Dwarf Inimitable, blotched and striped	Pelting	.65	8.00

PETUNIA—Continued.

Large-Flowering Sorts.

We call particular attention to our large-flowering strains of these, which are unsurpassed for size, shape and variety of colors.

		TEL. CIPHER.	OZ.
Large-Flowering, finest mixed	1-16 oz., $2.00	Pencil	$24.00
" " good quality, mixed	1/8 oz., 50c	Penciled	3.00
Fringed, mixed, extra choice	1/8 oz., 4.00	Pendant	
Giants of California, true	1-16 oz., 2.00	Pensive	24.00
Triumph of the Giants, the most beautiful strain of large flowering single petunia	1-16 oz. for 3.00	Pensively	
Ruffled Giants, extra choice	1-16 oz., 3.50	Pentact	
Pink	1-32 oz., 1.00	Pentink	
White	1-32 oz., 75c	Penture	
"Vaughan's Best" mixture of large flowering sorts includes all the above and others	1-16 oz., $2.50	People	

Double-Flowering Sorts.

Double Large-Flowering, extra choice mixed,	1,000 seeds, $1.00; 10,000 seeds, $9.00; 1-64 oz., $2.75; 1-32 oz., $5.00	Perfection
Double Large-Flowering, fringed, best mixed,	1,000 seeds, $1.00; 10,000 seeds, $9.00; 1-64 oz., $3.00	Period
Double Large-Flowering, good mixed	1-32 oz, $1.50	Perios
Lady of the Lake, double-fringed, pure white,	1,000 seeds, $1.20; 1-64 oz., $2.50	Permit
Double Fringed Perfection,	10,000 seeds, $9.00; 1,000 seeds, $1.00; 1-64 oz., $2.50	Perquisite
Double Fringed Pink	1,000 seeds, $1.60	Perfecto
"Vaughan's Special Mixture" Double, extra choice,	1,000 seeds, $1.20. 1-64 oz., $3.50	Perqueo

		OZ.	LB.
Phacelia Tenacetifolia, blue	Pewter	$0.10	$0.40

Pheasant's Eye Pink, see Dianthus Plumarius.

PHLOX.

RUMMONDI GRANDIFLORA.

White	Phase.
Pink	Pheasant.
Scarlet	Phenic.
Stellata Splendens	Phire.
Black Brown	Phiring.
Rosea Striata	Phirka.
Brilliant	Pew.
Carnea (Flesh)	Pheaton.
" **Violacea**	Phantasm
Rosea Aurea Stellata (Gold Star) oz., $1.00	Pharisee.
Alba **Oculata**	Phoca.
Coerulea Striata	Phocoid.
Scarlet **Striped**	Phœbe.
Yellow	Phonade.
Kermesina Splendens	Phonal.
Chamois **Rosa Alba** Oculata	Pewit.
Orbicularis Atrorosea	Phalanx.
" **Purpurea**	Phantom.

Each of above, except those priced above, per oz., 60c.; lb., $6.50.

PHLOX Cuspidata

PLATYCODON

PHLOX—Continued.

	TEL. CIPHER.	OZ.	LB.
Best Large-Flowering, Mixed	Phos	$0.40	$4.50
Imported Collection, 6 varieties, ea., 15c, net.	Pholobo		
Imported Collection, 12 varieties, ea., 25c, net.	Pholoboxe		
Phlox Drummondi, fine mixed	Phosphor	.35	3.80
Double Yellow, Isabellina semi-plena	Phrase	1.00	
" **White**, Alba semi-plena	Phrenic	.75	9.00
" **Red**, Atropurpurea semi-plena	Pholopur	1.70	
" **Mixed, the** above and others	Phro	.90	12.00
Star of Quedlinburg (Star Phlox), mixed	Phron	.45	5.00
Nana Compacta, mixed	Phycis	$1.00	$14.00
" " Snowball	Phylarc	1.80	
" " Fireball	Phyllula	1.50	
New Large-Flowering "Cecily," mixed	Phial	1.00	14.00
Hortensia-Flowered, extra choice, mixed	Physac	.60	6.50
" " white	Phylofa	.70	
" " scarlet	Phylogen	1.00	
" " brilliant rose	Phyloka	.70	
" " Salmon rose	Phyloked	1.00	
Vaughan's Special Mixture, includes all the varieties listed above and others	Physiol	.75	9.00
Decussata, perennial varieties, mixed	Physique	.60	7.00
Physalis Francheti, Chinese Lantern Plant	Packet	.25	3.00
Physostegia Virginica, pink	Physical	.40	
Virginica Alba, white	Physicon	.70	

Pinks, Chinese and others, see Dianthus.

	TEL. CIPHER.	OZ.	LB.
Platycodon Grandiflora, blue	Plat	$0.60	
Grandiflora Alba, white	Plateau	.65	
" Double Blue	Place	1.60	
" " White	Plaid	1.50	
Mariesi, blue	Plated	.65	
" fl. albo, white	Platen	.60	
" **Macranthum**	Platoon	1.20	
Polyanthus, mixed	Polyad	1.00	

POPPY—Papaver.

	TEL. CIPHER.	OZ.	LB.
American Flag, white with scarlet	Ponkate	$0.10	$0.65
Alpinum Laciniatum	Pomado	2.40	
Bracteatum	Pomfret	.15	1.25
Cornell, scarlet and white, double	Pomgater	.10	1.00
Danebrog, with large white spots	Pomp	.10	.40
Empress of China	Pomnarer	.10	1.20
Fairy Blush	Pomnta	.15	1.60
Golden Gate	Pomnzar	.15	1.60
Glaucum, Tulip Poppy, deep scarlet flowers	Pompous	.20	2.40
King Edward, new	Pomody	.25	2.50
Laevigatum, Persian or Firedragon	Pomquis	.15	1.40
Mephisto, deep scarlet with blackish violet spots	Pomras	.10	.40
Murselli fl. pl. Mikado, white; crimson striped	Pomsart	.10	.60
Nudicaule, Iceland yellow	Pomtary	.35	3.80
" album, white	Pomuare	.35	3.80
" **coccineum** (aurantiacum) scarlet	Pomvate	.40	5.00
" **striatum** striped	Pomway	.50	
" single mixed	Pomxary	.25	2.80
" **fl. pl.** double mixed, ¼ oz., 25c.	Pomyan	.80	
Orientale	Pomzence	.25	2.80
" Hybrids	Pond	.40	4.00
" **Princess Victoria Louise**	Pondat	1.20	
Paeoniflorum, Admiral	Poneate	.10	.60
" **fl. pl., paeonyfld.** double, white	Ponfer	.10	1.00
" " " " " yellow	Pongert	.10	1.00
" " " " " pink	Ponhair	.10	1.00
" " " " " scarlet	Ponile	.10	1.00
" " " " " mixed .. 10 lbs., $3.65	Ponjater	.10	.40
Pavoninum, Peacock brilliant-scarlet with glossy black ring	Ponlere	.25	2.60
Rhoeas single English scarlet	Ponmity	.20	2.00
" **fl. pl.** double **French mixed**	Ponnay	.10	.70
" **Shirley**	Ponope	.10	1.00
" Santa Rosa	Ponpape	.10	1.20
Somniferum single **Black Prince**	Ponquer	.25	2.50
" " **The Bride**, white	Ponryan	.10	.50
" **fl. pl.** double **Carnation**, Flowered, mixed .. 10 lbs., $3.50	Ponszat	.10	.40
" **nanum fl. pl.** Cardinale, scarlet	Pontal	.10	.60
" " " " **White Swan**	Ponuyon	.10	.60
Umbrosum, bright vermilion with black spots	Ponvatie	.10	.75
" **fl. pl.**, producing about 50 to 60% semi-double and double flowers	Ponwain	1.00	
Single Poppies, many sorts, mixed, 10 lbs., $3.00	Ponxent	.10	.35
Double Poppies, many sorts and colors, mixed	Ponzahn	.10	.60
Vaughan's Special **Mixture**, Single Poppies	Ponzater	.15	1.60
" " " Double Poppies	Ponzaton	.15	1.00
" " **Poppy Mixture**, includes all the double and single (annual varieties)	Ponzaster	.15	1.50

PORTULACA

Single Large-Flowering.

	TEL. CIPHER.	OZ.	LB.		TEL. CIPHER.	OZ.	LB.
White	Pottage	$0.20	$2.00	Scarlet	Potance	$0.20	$2.00
Pink	Portal	.20	2.00	**Striped**	Potanced	.20	2 00
Yellow	Potash	.20	2.00				

	TEL. CIPHER.	OZ.	LB.
Parana, New Giantflowered	Potancing	.80	
All colors mixed ... 5 lbs., $8.50	Potion	.15	1.80
Imported collection, 8 varieties...each, 15c, net	Portapo		

Double Large Flowering.

		TEL. CIPHER.				TEL. CIPHER.	
White	per ⅛ oz., 25c.	Pottage	$1.80	Pink	per ⅛ oz., 25c.	Pouch	$1.80
Yellow	per ⅛ oz., 25c.	Potter	1.80	Scarlet	per ⅛ oz., 25c.	Poultry	1.80

	TEL. CIPHER.	OZ.	LB.
Double Best Quality, Mixed	Pouncer	$1.25	$18.00
" **Good** " "	Praetor	.85	12.00
Imported collection, 6 varieties, double, each 25c.	Porthole		
Potentilla, Single mixed	Potent	.30	
" Double mixed	Potentate	1.60	
" Formosa, light red	Potential	.40	

PRIMULA CHINENSIS FIMBRIATA

Large-Flowering Fringed Sorts—ENGLISH GROWN.

			TEL. CIPHER.
Crimson King	1-32 oz.	$1.50	Prevent.
Queen Alexandra	1-32 oz.	1.75	Prevented.
Orange King	1-32 oz.	1.50	Primal.
Queen Mary, Rose Pink	1-32 oz.	2.00	Preventry.
Giant Pink	1-32 oz.	1.75	Presta.
His Majesty	1-32 oz.	1.50	Prevention.
Delicata	1-32 oz.	1.20	Prenal.
Covent Garden White	1-32 oz.	1.35	Prey.
Ruby Queen	1-32 oz.	1.50	Prick.
True Blue	1-32 oz.	1.75	Pretension.
Chiswick Red, Improved	1-32 oz.	1.75	Preterit.
Giant salmon	1-32 oz.	1.75	Principal.

Vaughan's International Primula Mixture, 1-16 oz., $3.25; ⅛ oz., $6.25; per oz., $45.00 .... Prison

Single Chinese Primrose, mixed colors, ⅛ oz., $1.00; oz., $6.00 .... Primary ..

PRIMULA—Continued.
Various Sorts.

		Tel. Cipher.	Oz.
Obconica Type	1-8 oz., $0.75	Present	$5.00
Gigantea Rosea, fine	1-32 oz., 1.75	Preserved	
" Kermesina	1-32 oz., 1.75	Prevervio	
Grandiflora, mixed	1-16 oz., .65	Preserve	8.00
" Kermesina	1-32 oz., 1.25	Presidium	
" Bright Rose	1-16 oz., .75	Preside	10.00
" Coerulea	1-32 oz., 1.00	Presided	
" White	1-16 oz., 1.00	Presidenity	12.00

Besides the above strains, we can supply "Special Florists" stock, grown by the most celebrated P. Obconica specialist. We will quote this strain on application.

		Tel. Cipher.	Oz.
Forbesi, Baby Primrose	⅛ oz., 50c	President	3.00
Japonica, mixed	¼ oz., 20c	Presume	.75
Kewensis	1-16 oz., $1.25	Previous	
Malacoides, new Improved Baby Primrose	⅛ oz., $1.25	Prevision	
Sieboldi, large flowered, new varieties	1-32 oz., 1.00	Pressant	
Veris Polyanthus (Cowslip), mixed		Press	1.00
" Coerulea	1,000 seeds, $4.00	Presidency	
" New Giant Flowered, choice	⅛ oz., 60c	Pretestine	3.00
" Gold Laced Varieties, choicest mixed		Presuming	2.50
Vulgaris, the true yellow Primrose		Presser	1.00

		Tel. Cipher.	Oz.	Lb.
Pueraria Thunbergiana, Kudzu Vine		Puerto	$0.40	$4.50
Pyrethrum Parthenifolium Aureum, Gold. Feather		Prestine	.15	1.85
Parthenifolium Aureum Selaginoides		Pyral	.30	
Roseum Hybridum, single mixed		Pyram	1.00	14.00
" " Grandiflorum, New Giant, mxd.		Pyrax	1.50	
" " dbl. mxd., choice	⅛ oz., $1.10	Pyrite	8.00	
" " Kelway's Hybrids		Pyx	4.50	
Uliginosum		Pyroe	1.00	
Rehmannia Angulata	⅛ oz., 50c	Repentant		
Rheum Palmatum Tanguticum		Rhomboid	.15	
Rhodanthe, mixed		Rhomb	.30	3.00
Ricinus Zanzibarensis, mixed	10 lbs., $4.75	Riches	.10	.50
" " **Enormis**		Riddance	.10	1.00
Borboniensis Arboreus		Ridpath	.10	.50
Sanguineus	10 lbs., $2.70	Riffler	.05	.30
Cambodgensis, very dark	5 lbs., $2.50	Rifle	.10	.55
Panormitanus		Ridpaned	.15	1.50
Mixed, many kinds	10 lbs., $2.50	Rigid	.05	.30
Romneya Coulteri, white, large		Roll	.75	
Rosa Polyantha Nana, "Baby Rose," clean seed		Rosetta	2.50	

"VAUGHAN'S SPECIAL MIXTURES"

Means the Best in Existence.

All of "Vaughan's Special Mixtures" are made up by ourselves from separate colors and specially fine strains, combined in desirable proportions. We spare no trouble or expense to secure for them the newest and choicest sorts, the widest possible range of shade and color. Vaughan's Special Mixtures" are full of life. We pride ourselves upon them, and our customers may depend upon it that any mixture listed as "Vaughan's Special Mixture" is the best of its kind in existence.

SALVIA SPLENDENS Clara Bedman

	TEL. CIPHER.	OZ.	LB.
Rudbeckia Bicolor Superba, large	Rudbec	$0.20	$2.00
" " " semi-plena	Rudbock	.50	
Fulgida, yellow, very free	Rude	.50	
Newmani, bright yellow, very free and lasting	Rudiment	.60	
Nitida, Autumn Glory ....1-16 oz., 80c.	Ruffian		
Purpurea (Echinacea)	Rueful	1.40	
" Grandiflora	Ruff	1.80	
Laciniata, yellow	Rudy	.15	
Salpiglossis Variabilis, mixed	Saber	.25	3.00
Large-flowering, extra choice mixed	Sad	.35	4.00
"**Emperor,**" mixed, very fine	Sadness	.85	10.00
Crimson .... ⅛ oz., 25c.	Sadden	1.60	
Faust .... ⅛ oz., 25c.	Saddle	1.60	
Lilac and Gold .... ⅛ oz., 25c.	Saddler	1.60	
Pink .... ⅛ oz., 25c.	Saddlery	1.60	
Purple Violet and Gold .... ⅛ oz., 25c.	Sadducee	1.60	
Purple Velvety Violet .... ⅛ oz., 25c.	Sadly	1.60	
Golden Yellow .... ⅛ oz., 25c.	Safe	1.60	
Vaughan's Special Mixture	Sadiron	1.60	
Salvia Splendens (Scarlet Sage)	Safety	.90	12.00
" Clara Bedman or Bonfire	Sailed	1.35	18.00
" "**Drooping Spikes,**" very fine	Salad	1.50	20.00
" **Fireball,** new extra choice	Salt	2.00	28.00
" Zurich	Saloon	3.00	40.00
" Mixed	Sailor	1.50	
Patens, blue .... ¼ oz., 60c.	Salmon	2.20	
Coccinea, scarlet, annual Flowering Sage	Salvable	.20	2.00
Argentea, silver-leaved	Salvage	.20	2.00
Farinacea, blue	Salvation	.60	
Santolina Maritima	Salamander	.40	
Sanvitalia Procumbens fl. pl	Salvigold	.30	
Saponaria Ocymoides Splendens	Sapona	.20	
Caucasia fl. pl	Sappa	.70	

	TEL. CIPHER.	OZ.	LB.
Scabiosa, Double Dwarf, mixed	Scales	$0.15	$1.25
Large Flowering, Double Tall, mixed	Scallop	.25	2.80
Atropurpurea Major, Tall, mixed	Scalpel	.15	1.25
Snowball, best double white	Scamper	.20	2.00
Double Fiery Scarlet	Scanty	.50	
" Black Prince	Scarcity	.50	
" Mauve (Azure Fairy)	Scamp	.50	
" Pink	Scan	.50	
" Yellow (minor aurea pl.)	Scatter	.25	
Caucasica, lilac, perennial	Scheme	.85	10.00
" Alba, white, very fine	Scabra	2.00	
Japonica	Socket	1.50	
Schizanthus, (Butterfly Flower) mixed	Scoul	.10	1.00
Hybridus Grandiflorus	Scowler	.60	
Wisetonensis, new ... 1-32 oz., 85c.	Scowling		
Sedum Coeruleum (Stone Crop)	Sedum	2.00	
Shamrock	Silicic	.30	
Senecio Elegans fl. pl., double mixed	Senecio	.35	4.00
Sensitive **Plant** (Mimosa Pudica)	Minstrel	.15	1.80
Silene Pendula Alba	Silice	.10	.65
" " Rosea	Silros	.10	.65
Orientalis, perennial, beautiful dark rose	Siek	.10	
Armeria (Catchfly), mixed	Silry	.10	.60
Smilax, new crop	Smilax	.15	1.80
Snapdragon, see Antirrhinum.			
Solanum **Capsicastrum Nanum**, Jerusalem **Cherry**	Sorrow	.20	2.00
Capsicastrum **Melvini**	Sorrowal	1.50	
Stachys Lanata	Somber	.15	
Statice, Latifolia	Station	.50	6.00
Sinuata, blue, fine cut fl., used largely in Eng	Stationary	.10	1.00
Stevia Serrata	Stevia	.50	
Lindleyana, a clearer white than Serrata	Stiffe	.70	

STOCKS.

Large-Flowering Double Dwarf German Ten Weeks.

Our Stock Seed is from one of the best European Growers and is unexcelled, it is just the quality florists want.

	TEL. CIPHER.
Crimson	Stockade.
Blood-Red	Stocky.
Brilliant Rose	Stoical.
White	Stoker.
Canary Yellow	Stolzcup.
Dark Blue	Stooping.
Light Blue	Stoop.
Flesh	Stooped.

Each of above, ⅛ oz., 20c; ¼ oz., 35c; oz., $1.25; lb., $16.00.

Extra Choice Mixed, all colors, oz., $1.00; lb., $14.00. Stoppage.
Good mixed, oz., 60c; lb., $6.00 .... Storage.

Imported Collection, Large-Flowering Ten Weeks Stocks of 12 varieties, each, 30c net............ Straight.

STOCKS Beauty of Nice

Imported Collection, Large-Flowering Ten Weeks Stocks of 6 varieties........each, 15c, net..Strain ....

STOCKS—Continued.

	TEL. CIPHER.	OZ.	LB.
Giant Perfection, light blue	Stockful	$1.40	$20.00
" " flesh color	Stockley	1.60	
" " scarlet	Stockroom	1.60	
" " pink	Stockwork	1.40	20.00
" " sky-blue	Soloist	1.60	
" " dark blue	Solsat	1.60	
" " white (Princess Alice)	Story	1.25	16.00
" " canary yellow	Stout	2.00	
" " mixed (Cut and Come again)	Stork	1.00	14.00
Imported Collection of 6 varieties, each, 30c net.	Stocking.		
Prince Bismarck, white	Stow.	2.00	
" " lavender	Stoway	2.80	
" " Gold Ball	Stowedy	3.00	
Beauty of Nice, pink	Stomach	1.00	14.00
" " **white**	Stop	.80	
" " Crimson King	Strainer	1.20	
" Queen Alexandra	Stockstill	1.20	16.00
" " **Monte Carlo** (Creole), canary yellow	Stockton	1.60	
" **Cote d'Azure,** violet blue	Stocktane	2.50	
" " **Abundance,** delicate rosy lilac	Stockum	2.50	
" " **Mont Blanc**	Stocklum	2.40	
White Column, fine white ... ⅛ oz., 50c.	Stouten	3.00	
Crimson Column ... ⅛ oz., 50c.	Stoic	3.00	
Snowflake, early white, forcing ... ⅛ oz., $1.25.	Straggle	9.00	
Vaughan's Fire Flame ... ⅛ oz., 45c.	Strive	3.20	
Emperor or Winter, mixed ... ⅛ oz., 45c.	Stroy	3.00	
" " white ... ⅛ oz., 60c.	Stroying	3.50	
" " rose ... ⅛ oz., 60c.	Stoniness	3.50	
" crimson ... ⅛ oz., 60c.	Stood	3.50	
" " Emp. Elizabeth ... ⅛ oz., 60c.	Straykant	3.50	
Vaughan's Special Mixture	Stored	2.50	

	TEL. CIPHER.	OZ.	LB.
Stokesia Cyanea, Stokes' Aster	Stokes	.85	10.00
" " Alba	Stokers	1.00	
Streptocarpus, Largest New Hybrids ... 1-32 oz., $1.25.	Strepts		

SUNFLOWER.

	TEL. CIPHER.	OZ.	LB.
Sunflower, Miniature (Cucumerifolius)	Summons	.10	1.00
Cucumerifolius Albus, white	Sunflora	.15	1.60
" **"Stella"**	Sunbeam	.15	1.40
" **"Orion"**	Sunbird	.15	1.40
" **Double Hybrids**	Sunder	.20	2.20
" Perkeo, dwarf	Sumpter	.15	1.60
" Special Mixed	Sundered	.20	2.00
Many-Flowered, double	Sundial	.15	1.60
Argyrophyllus (Silver-leaved)	Sundry	.10	.60
Californicus fl. pl., double California	Sunset	.10	.70
Globosus Fistulosus fl. pl., fine double	Sunshine	.10	.70
Double Dwarf, (Nanus fl. pl.)	Super	.10	.85
Double Chrysanthemum-Flowered	Superba	.10	1.20
Double, all kinds mixed	Suppine	.10	.70
Vaughan's Special Mixture, all the above	Supple	.15	1.80
Maximiliani (Missouricus)	Sung	.60	
Perennial Hybrids, mixed	Supreme	2.00	

VAUGHAN'S SWEET PEAS

Our Sweet Peas are raised by careful growers, who are specialists in this line, and better seed cannot be had in this country than is supplied by Vaughan's Seed Store.

The Grandiflora types may have a small percentage of rogues, if any. When it comes to the Spencer types, however, it is too well known they are not so well established as to be as true as the Grandiflora or Unwin types.

As mentioned above, our seed is grown by the most careful growers, rogued and selected, and represents the best in existence of these strains; but we cannot be held responsible for whatever rogues or sports that may appear in the seeds we supply.

The following prices are f. o. b. Chicago and are subject to change without notice.

SPENCER VARIETIES

	Tel. Cipher	Lb.
Apple-Blossom, crimson pink and white, shaded	Seil	$2 00
Asta Ohn, lavender tinted with mauve	Seiminal	3 25
Aurora, orange rose, striped on white	Selation	2 00
Blanche Ferry, pink and white	Senatorial	3 50
Captain of the Blues, standard purple; wings blue	Siegtar	2 00
Clara Curtis, primrose	Sign	
Countess of Spencer Hybrids	Smart	1 25
Countess of Spencer Variety, true pale pink, darker edge	Smash	2 25
Dainty, white with pink picotee edge	Soda	
Duplex Spencer Cream Pink. The standard and wings are a rich cream-pink, and practically all the plants give flowers with double or triple standards	Sodarty	
Ethel Roosevelt, rose pink, primrose ground	Spaniard	
Evelyn Hemus, buff ground with rosy picotee edge	Spanish	
Flora Norton, bright blue with slight tint of purple	Speak	2 75
Florence Morse, delicate blush, with pink margin	Spearade	2 25
Florence Nightingale, lavender	Spank	
George Herbert, standard rosy magenta, wings deep carmine	Specialty	2 50
George Washington, glorious crimson-scarlet self	Spear	1 50
Helen Lewis or Orange Countess	Spin	
John Ingman, same as George Herbert		
King Edward VII, the best of the rich red sorts	Sportive	2 25
Marie Corelli, rose carmine, tinted cherry red	Spanker	3 50
Mrs. Hugh Dickson, pale salmon pink on cream ground	Spanking	5 00
Mrs. Routzahn, apricot, suffused with pink	Stampade	3 50
Othello, dark rich deep maroon	Stay	2 50

SPENCER VARIETIES—Continued

	Tel. Cipher.	Lb.
Pearl-Gray, Pearl or dove-gray, suffused with light rose	Stayyed	$
Primrose, true primrose color	Steilery	2 50
Senator, claret and chocolate stripes on light heliotrope ground	Stocking	2 50
Tennant, purplish mauve	Stoical	3 50
Vermilion Brilliant, brilliant scarlet	Stoje	
White, pure white Spencer	Street	3 00
W. T. Hutchins, apricot and lemon, overlaid blush	Streator	3 00
Vaughan's Special Mixture of Spencer Varieties	Stattary	2 50

UNWIN AND GRANDIFLORA TYPES

	Tel. Cipher.	Lb.
America, the brightest blood-red, striped white	Seide	75
Aurora, orange rose, striped on white	Sein	75
Black Knight, dark maroon	Seligman	75
Blanche Ferry, pink and white	Senat	60
Bolton's Pink, pink shaded rose	Sense	45
Captain of the Blues, purplish mauve	Sieg	75
Countess of Radnor, superseded by Lady Grisel Hamilton	Sod	
Cupid, Mixed	Silchmix	40
Dainty, white, with pink edge, unique	Soldat	75
David R. Williamson, rich indigo blue	Soldier	60
Dorothy Eckford, one of the best whites	Soll	50
Dorothy Tennant, deep rose mauve	Somit	70
Duke of Westminster, deep rose maroon, overlaid with bright shining violet	Sopha	75
Emily Henderson, white, early and free	Span	50
E. J. Castle, rich carmine rose, with salmon shading in the standard	Spangle	80
Evelyn Byatt, fine orange salmon	Sparrow	70
Frank Dolby, largest and finest pale blue	Spatula	60
Flora Norton, a very bright blue	Spatz	75
Gladys Unwin, pale rosy pink	Spearfish	80
Helen Pierce, blue, with dark grain markings	Spinley	70
Henry Eckford, of extraordinary orange color	Spinster	
Hon. Mrs. E. Kenyon, yellow	Spink	60
King Edward VII, Special selection; especially fine	Sported	60
Lady Grisel Hamilton, best of all lavender sorts	Spreu	60
Lord Nelson, deeper and richer than Navy Blue; same as Brilliant Blue	Spring	85
Lottie Eckford, white, suffused lavender	Sprintz	60
Lovely, soft shell pink	Spule	1 00
Maid of Honor, white, edged lavender	Staar	75
Miss Willmott, richest orange pink, shaded rose	Stafel	70
Mrs. A. Watkins, large pale pink	Standard	70

UNWIN AND GRANDIFLORA TYPES—Continued.

	Tel. Cipher	Lb.
Mrs. Geo. Higginson, Jr., delicate light blue	Stallman	$1 00
Mrs. Walter Wright, beautiful mauve color	Statt	75
Navy Blue, deep violet blue	Statthaf	1 00
Nora Unwin, giant white	Stattin	1 20
Othello, abeautiful dark brown chocolate-red color	Stattlich	65
Prima Donna, soft pink	Steil	75
Princer of Wales, a bright rose, self, of intense colo and fine form and substance	Stehend	65
Queen Alexandra, giant size scarlet	Stellate	75
Rose du Barri, salmon rose and orange	Stale	75
Romolo Piazanni, true violet, blue	Stullify	
Saint George, brilliant orange scarlet	Steele	1 10
Salopian, one of the best of the dark bright reds	Stimme	75
Senator, chocolate, striped white	Stock	60
Unique, white, flaked with light blue	Stratum	60
White Wonder, the many-flowered white	Streams	65

CHRISTMAS or WINTER-FLOWERING SWEET PEAS

	Tel. Cipher	Lb.
Canary Bird, early yellow	Seimke	$1 00
Christmas Countess / **Mrs. C. H. Totty** } sky blue	Spiral	1 00
Christmas Pink / **Earliest of All** } pink and white	Siesta	85
Christmas Meteor, brilliant red	Strebe	1 00
Christmas Prima Donna / **Mrs. F. J. Delansky** } daybreak pink	Seed	1 00
Christmas White / **Mont Blanc** / **Florence Denzer** } pure white	Signal	70
Mrs. Alexander Wallace, lavender	Standery	1 50
Mrs. E. Wild, bright rose	Stella	75
Mrs. W. W. Smalley / **Mrs. William Sim** } salmon pink	Starost	85
Snowbird / **Burpee's Earliest White** } black-seeded white	Sensitive	60
Winter-Flowering Sweet Peas Mixed	Sentence	75

SWEET PEAS IN MIXTURE

Vaughan's Prize Mixture—Stumpf. This mixture contains the cream of the new and standard sorts, including most of the new Spencer varieties. It is made up entirely of separate named sorts, carefully proportioned as to its composition, and we can safely say **"there is no better mixture in existence,"** no matter at what price or under what name it may be offered. **Per lb. $1.00, 10 lbs. $9.50, 100 lbs. $90.00.**

Vaughan's Florists' Mixture—Stumpfsinn. This is a mixture made by ourselves, of principally light-colored varieties, suitable for florists' cut-flower trade. It is a very carefully proportioned mixture and gives satisfaction. **Per lb. $1.00, per 10 lbs. $9.50.**

Eckford Mixture—Stunde. This mixture contains over thirty varieties, including some of the novelties of 1911 and other choice sorts. **Per lb. 70c, 10 lbs. $6.50, 100 lbs. $60.00.**

All Colors Mixed—Sturm. Also a very good mixture. Contains over twenty varieties. **Per lb. 60c, 100 lbs. $50.00.**

	TEL. CIPHER.	OZ.	LB.
Sweet Sultan, mixed	Supply	$0.10	$1.20
Yellow (Centaurea Suaveolens)	Cement	.25	2.80
Sweet Violet, Semperflorens, blue	Sweeper	.75	9.00
The Czar	Sweeten	1.25	
Sweet William, single mixed ... 5 lbs., $4.75	Swell	.10	1.00
Mammoth-Flowered, single mixed	Swelter	.30	3.50
" " double mixed	Swift	.75	12.00
Double white	Swiftness	.60	
" Blood-red (Atrosanguineus pl.)	Swiger	1.00	14.00
" mixed	Swinburn	.45	5.00
" Auricula-Flowered, best mixed	Swing	.50	6.00
" roseus, double pink	Swingest	1.50	
Single Auricula-Flowered, best mixed	Swinger	.10	1.20
" Diadematus	Swipe	1.50	
" Carmine Beauty	Swiss	4.00	
" Roseus, "Pink Beauty"	Swin	.90	
" Blood-red (Atrosanguineus)	Swiping	.15	1.80
" Albus	Swiper	.20	1.80
" Sutton's Scarlet	Swiped	4.00	
" Johnson's Giant	Swissert	.50	6.00
" Nigrescens, darkest sort	Swissing	.15	
" Salmoneus, salmon	Swissed	1.20	
" Harlequin Mutabilis	Swivel	.15	1.80
Vaughan's Special Mixture	Switch	.60	7.00
Thalictrum Adiantifolium	Thermal	1.25	
Thunbergia, mixed	Thorax	.35	4.00
Torenia Fournieri Grandiflora ... 1/8 oz., 25c.	Torment	1.40	
" White Wings ... 1/8 oz., 25.	Torpedo	1.40	
" Bailloni ... 1/8 oz., 50c.	Torpilz		
Tritoma Grandiflora, new hybrids, mixed	Tritoma	.50	

TROPÆOLUM LOBBIANUM—LOBB'S NASTURTIUM.

		1/4 LB.	LB
Asa Gray, yellowish white	Transmit	$0.15	$0.40
Black Prince	Trance	.15	.50
Emma Alida ... oz., 25c.	Tranquil	.75	2.50
Princess Victoria Louise, cream white, orange-scarlet blotches; calyx and spur orange-red	Trawler	.15	.45
Lili Smith, scarlet	Transpose	.15	.45
Spitfire, brilliant scarlet	Trapper	.15	.40
Regina, salmon, extra fine	Tropical	.15	.60
Giant of Battles, sulphur with red	Travel	.15	.40
Brilliant, dark scarlet	Traveler	.15	.45
Cardinal, dark scarlet	Traver	.15	.45
Golden Queen, golden yellow	Trawling	.15	.40
Lucifer, very dark scarlet	Tray	.15	.50
Napoleon III, golden yellow, spotted with brown	Trazer	.15	.40
Queen Wilhelmina	Tread	.20	.80
Queen Alexandra, flowers blood red	Traverse	.25	1.00
" **of the Morning,** flowers aurora colored	Treiste	.20	.80
" **Emma,** flowers scarlet	Treadest	.15	.60
" **of Spain,** flowers golden yellow	Transform	.20	.80
Fimbriatum, fringed flowers	Transfer	.15	.60
"Queen type" (var. leaved sorts) mixed	Trawl	.20	.60
King of the Blacks, black-brown	Treading	.15	.45
Firefly, flowers dark orange, spotted and flamed blood-red; spur blood-red; foliage and stems dark	Treasure	.15	.50
Ivy Leaf, scarlet	Treatise	.15	1.00
Princess Juliana, new ... oz., 75c.	Tremulous	3.00	
Primrose, creamy-white with brown spots	Tremor	.15	.45
Virchow, deep ruby rose	Tropico	.15	.45
Many Colors Mixed. 100 lbs., $30.00; 10 lbs., $3.20	Tropoci	.10	.35

		OZ.
Valeriana Rubra, Garden Heliotrope	Vase	$0.20
" " flore albo	Vasal	.20

VERBENA "VAUGHAN'S BEST" MIXTURE. "Verbest."

This is unquestionably the best strain of Verbena seed in existence. It is composed of the choicest strains and colors of the Mammoth type, the best European introductions of late years, all grown separately and mixed by us in the right proportion. Per oz., $1.00; per lb., $14.00.

	TEL. CIPHER.	OZ.	LB.
Verbena hybrida, **Defiance**, brilliant scarlet, true	Veinage	$0.75	$9.00
Firefly, brilliant scarlet, white eye	Vein	.90	12 00
Mammoth, mixed	Velveteen	.50	6.00
" **White**, extra choice	Vemager	.50	6.50
" Rose and Carmine shades	Vemend	.65	8.00
" Purple shades	Venal	.60	7.50
Italian Striped	Vengar	.60	6.50
Striped, white on red ground, very fine	Vengeance	.90	12.00
Auricula-Flowered, mixed	Vengeful	.50	6.00
Mayflower, beautiful pink	Vengehard	.90	12.00
Gigantea, new giant flowered in splendid mixture	Venison	2.00	
Scarlet, white eye	Venice	1.25	
Purple, white eye	Venitian	1.25	
Dark Blue, white eye	Venhog	.60	6.50
Purple Mantle	Venial	.60	
Lutea, yellow	Venom	.60	
Good Mixed	Vent	.30	3.50
Fine Mixed	Venture	.40	4.50
Extra Choice Mixed	Verdan	.50	6.00
Nana Compacta, white	Verb	1.50	
" " scarlet	Verbatum	1.50	
" " scarlet with white eye	Venue	2.00	
" " Dwarf mixed	Verdure	.85	10.00
Venosa	Verify	.25	3.00
Lemon (Citriodora)	Vernal	1.20	16.00
Erinoides, Moss Verbena, purple	Vernest	.40	
" white	Vernole	.40	
Veronica Spicata	Viands	.45	
Vinca **Rosea**, mixed	Vibrate	.35	4.00
Rosea, pink	Vicae	.40	4.00
" Fl. Albo, white with pink eye	Victim	.40	4.50
" Alba Pura, pure white	Victor	.40	4.50
Viola Cornuta, mixed	Vide	.50	6.00
Admiration, dark blue	Victory	.80	
Golden Yellow	Victual	.50	
Pure White (White Perfection)	Vie	.80	
Blue Perfection	Vigil	.80	
Viola Odorata, see Sweet Violet.			
Virginia Stocks, mixed ... 5 lbs., $2.35	Vigilant	.10	.50
Viscaria, mixed	Viscaria	.10	1.00
Wahlenbergia, see Platycodon.			
Wallflower, Single mixed	Wall	.10	1.00
Parisian Forcing, bloom the first year	Walloping	.15	1.40
Double Mixed, extra choice	Water	1.80	24.00
New annual blood-red	Watering	.30	
Whitlavia Gloxinoides	Whirl	.10	
Wild Cucumber ... 10 lbs., $8.50	Wilder	.10	1.00
Wistaria sinensis	Winsiter	.20	2.00

ZINNIA—Crested and Curled

WILD CUCUMBER

	TEL. CIPHER.	oz	lb
Xeranthemum, double mixed	Xenia	$0.20	$2.40
Zea Japonica fol. var., Variegated Maize	Zealand	.05	.25
" " Quadricolor Perfecta	Zealate	.10	1.20
Zinnia Elegans, Double White	Zealot	.20	2.00
" " Scarlet	Zebra	.20	2.00
" " Golden Yellow	Zed	.20	2.00
" " Pink	Zinkite	.20	2.00
" " Flesh color	Zedlick	.20	2.00
" " Double mixed. 5 lbs., $6.50	Zingle	.15	1.40
Jacqueminot	Zinhate	.25	2.60
Double Dwarf (Pumila fl. pl.), Mxd., extra	Zion	.20	2.00
" " White (Snowball)	Zionist	.30	3.00
" " Scarlet (Fireball)	Zionate	.30	3.00
Robusta Plenissima, mixed, double, ex. large	Zither	.25	2.50
" " Queen Victoria, white	Zone	.30	3.50
" " or Colossal White	Zodiacul	.75	
" " Colossal Golden Yellow	Zoographer	.75	
" " Colossal Scarlet	Zoonomy	.75	
Zebra or Carnation Striped	Zodiac	.30	3.00
Gracillima coccinea pl. (Red Riding Hood)	Zodactor	.65	8.00
Crested and Curled	Zonal	.25	2.80
Double Pompone (Darwin), mixed	Zouave	.25	2.80
Double Liliput, mixed	Zonay	.25	2.80
Mexicana (Haageana) fl. pl	Zygenea	.40	
" **Hybrida**, new Mexican Hybrids	Zymo	.75	
Wild Flower Garden Mixture, 100 lbs., $25.00; 10 lbs. $2.70	Winter		.30
Mixture of Annuals, for open ground sowing, tall sorts, 10 lbs., $2.75	Wintercold		.30
Mixture of Annuals, for open ground sowing, semi-dwarf sorts, 10 lbs., $3.75	Wintering		.40
Mixture of Annuals, for open ground sowing, dwarf sorts, 10 lbs., $4.00	Winterish		.45
Mixture of Annuals, for open ground sowing, for bees, 10 lbs., $4.50	Winterox		.50

SUMMER FLOWERING BULBS, ETC.

Special Prices on Large Quantities

SINGLE TUBEROUS ROOTED BEGONIA

AMARYLLIS.	TEL. CIPHER.	DOZ.	100
Belladonna Major	Amaree	$1.25	$8.00
Formosissima	Amar	.50	3.50
Johnsoni, 7 to 9 inch	Amarrer	1.85	15.00
" 9 to 11 inch	Amarroy	2.50	22.00
Apios Tuberosa	Amas	.25	1.50

BEGONIAS, Tuberous Rooted. Giant Flowering Varieties

	TEL. CIPHER.	DOZ.	100	1000
Single white	Begul	$0.35	$2.25	$20.00
Single Yellow	Beguine	.35	2.25	20.00
Single Scarlet	Belier	35	2.25	20.00
Single Pink	Bellette	.35	2.25	20.00
Single Mixed	Belledone	.25	2.00	18.00
Double White	Bellot	.55	3.50	30.00
Double Yellow	Bemol	.55	3.50	30.00
Double Scarlet	Benarde	.55	3.50	30.00
Double Pink	Benet	.55	3.50	30.00
Double Mixed	Benin	.50	3.25	28.00
Cardinal (single)	Berao	1.50	....	.....
Lafayette	Beron	1.25	....	.....
Graf Zeppelin	Best	1.00	....	.....
Cristata	Bester	1.00	....	.....
Bertini	Bestone	1.00	....	.....
Chlidanthus Fragrans	Calious	.40	2.75	25.00
Cinnamon Vine.—Mailing size	Calepin	.25	1.50	12.00
" " Extra size	Calir	.35	2.25	18.00

GLOXINIAS.

	Doz.	100	1,000
Named sorts in following colors: Scarlet, Pure White, Blue with White Throat and Red with White Border	.45	3.00	27.00
Mixed Colors	.40	2.75	25.00

SUMMER FLOWERING BULBS (Continued).

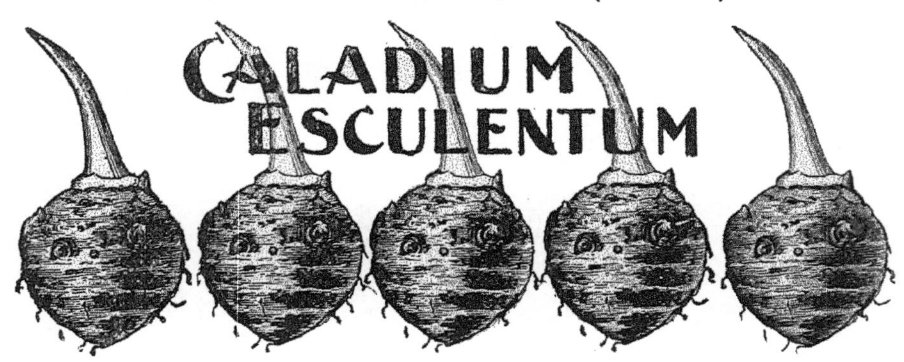

CALADIUM ESCULENTUM, or Elephant's Ear.

Cured and sound bulbs with good, live center shoots.		Doz.	100	1,000
5 to 7 inches in circumference	Calamine	$0.25	$1.50	$12.00
7 to 9 " "	Calandre	.45	2.75	24.00
[illegible] to 11 " "	Calcaire	.75	5.25	47.00
11 to 12 "	Calcon	1.25	8.50	75.00
12 inches and up	Calciner	1.75	12.00	

Ten per cent. discount from above when shipped from New York Store.

	TEL. CIPHER.	DOZ.	100.	1000.
Fern Balls, 5 inches in diameter	Gab	$1.80	14.00	.....
" " 7 inches in diameter	Gaber	2.80	22.00	.....
Hyacinthus Candicans, 1-2 inches	Gaze	.25	1.35	10.00
" " 2-3 inches	Gazer	.30	1.50	12.00
Ismene Calathina	Gazism	.75	5.00	.....
Madeira Vine Roots, 2-3 inches	Liberal	.20	1.30	9.00
" " " 3 inch up	Liberaler	.25	1.40	11.00
Montbretia, Mixed	Libertin	.25	1.35	10.00
Oxalis, White, Pink and Red			.25	1.25
Richardia Alba Maculata, Spotted Calla	Ligne	.45	3.00	25.00
" **Elliottiana,** yellow Calla	Lighter	2.00	15.00	.....
Tigridias Sep., colors	Lijaba	.45	3.00	25.00
Tigridias, mixed	Lijab	.35	2.00	18.00
Zephyranthus Candida	Zephcan	.25	1.50	12.00
Zephyranthus Rosea	Zephcanea	.45	3.00	25.00

Well Cured Bulbs. **TUBEROSES.** Free from Rot

	TEL. CIPHER.	100.	1.000.
True Excelsior Pearl, 1st Class, as received from our growers			
" " " " in Chicago	Rose	$1.00	$8.50
" " " " in New York	Rosebif	.90	8.00
Hand picked after March 1st	Roseat	1.15	9.00
" " " **Mammoth,** 6 to 8 inches	Rosman	1.75	15.00
" " " **mailing size**	Rosear	.50	4.50
" " " " " in New York	Roseau	.45	4.00
Variegated **Leaved,** single	Rosier	1.50	12.00
Albino, early single white	Rostre	1.50	12.00
Armstrong's Ever Blooming	Rotule	1.75	15.00

SUMMER FLOWERING BULBS

HARDY LILIES

PLEASE NOTE—Japan Lily Bulbs usually arrive in this country with a large percentage of them rotten and entirely worthless. We repack all of this stock before shipping and bulbs will be in sound condition when leaving our store.

Prices below subject to change without notice.

We furnish 25 of a kind at the 100 rate, less at the dozen rate.

	TEL. CIPHER.	DOZ.	100.	1000.
Auratum, 8 to 9 inches	Limbe	$0.75	$5.00	$45.00
" 9 to 11 inches	Lime	1.25	8.25	75.00
Rubrum (Speciosum), 8 to 9 inches	Liserer	.65	4.75	42.50
" " 9 to 11 inches	Liset	1.00	7.00	
" " 11 to 13 inches	Lisoth	1.35	9.50	
Album " 8 to 9 inches scarce	Litas	1.25	8.00	
" " 9 to 11 inches	Litato	1.50	11.50	
Melpomene " 8 to 9 inches	Liter	.75	5.00	45.00
" " 9 to 11 inches	Liton	1.00	7.50	70.00
Canadense	Lourer	.60	4.00	
Pardalinum	Lou	.75	5.00	
Superbum	Lourd	.60	4.00	
Tenuifolium	Loup	.75	5.00	
Tigrinum Splendens, Improved Single Tiger	Literary	.45	2.75	24.00
" Fl. Pl., Double Tiger Lily	Lizard	.50	3.50	30.00
Umbellatum	Lout	.60	4.00	
Lily of the Valley Clumps	Louter	2.50	20.00	

LILY BULBS AND VALLEY FROM ICE STORAGE

These are Chicago storage prices. Customers of our New York house will please ask for prices there. Our cases are numbered and "stock marked," and these records show on your invoice. You can thus "Repeat" your orders with assurance of receiving the same grade and packing. Try us. Book now for future dates and secure your supply.

VALLEY LONDON MARKET

Packed 500 Pips to case	$ [illegible].00
Packed 1,000 Pips to case	15.00
Packed 2,000 Pips to case	28.00

Lilium Rubrum

	Per case
8-9 inch (160 Bulbs to case)	$7.25
9-11 inch (100 Bulbs to case)	7.00

Lilium Auratum

	Per case
8-9 inch (160 Bulbs to case)	$8.00
9-11 inch (100 Bulbs to case)	7.50

Lilium Album

	Per case
8-9 inch (160 Bulbs to case)	$12.75
9-11 inch (100 Bulbs to case)	11.50

Lil Giganteum

	Per case
7-9 inch (300 Bulbs to case)	$17.00
9-10 inch (200 Bulbs to case)	16.50

KUNDERDI "GLORY"

GLADIOLUS
KUNDERDI "GLORY"

WITH "RUFFLED" PETALS

The broadly expanded, wide open flowers, paired by twos, all face in the same direction and are carried on straight stout stalks, fully 3½ feet. From three to eight of these handsome flowers are open at one time. Each petal is exquisitely ruffled and fluted.

The color is a delicate cream pink, with a most attractive crimson stripe in the center of each lower petal, the shade of which is unique in Gladioli. The ruffling of the petals in this new strain has attracted much attention the country over.

Price—Per 100, $5.00; per 1000, $43.00 (250 bulbs at the 1000 rate); lots of 3000 at **$40.00 per 1000.**

Code Word "Garg."

GLADIOLUS PRINCEPS.

The flowers are 5 to 6 in. broad, the petals are very wide and rounded, well reflexed, forming an almost circular flower. The color is brilliant scarlet-crimson, carrying mostly three broad white blotches on the lower petals.

Price—First Size Bulbs, per 100, $8.00. Second Size Bulbs, per 100, $6.75. Code Word, "Garcia."

GLADIOLUS, MRS. FRANCIS KING.

The long, strong flower stalks with foliage, and its effective flower spike with a good line of reserve buds continually opening, and with flower 4½ inches across, and five to six flowers well spread out on the spike at the same time, gives for vases, in hotel lobbies and dining rooms, parlor decorations, etc., an effect not produced by any other Gladiolus. The color, brilliant Flamingo pink blazed with vermilion red, is most effective both in daylight and under artificial light. **First size, per 100, $1.75; per 1000, $16.00.**
Second size, per 100, $1.50; per 1000, $14.00.

Code Word "Gam."

GLADIOLUS AMERICA. Code Word—Gladamer.

Soft lavender pink, very light, almost a tinted white, spikes two and three feet long, very large spreading blooms and luxuriant dark green foliage. When cut it lasts in water a week or more, the blossoms retaining their vigor and delicate coloring to the last.

First size, per 100, $2.75; 1000 for $24.00.
Second size, 1 to ⅜ ins., per 100, $2.50; per 1000, $21.00.

CHICAGO WHITE.

The flowers are well expanded, well placed upon the stalk, pure white with faint lavender streaks in the lower petals. In form they resemble the Childsii type. They are borne on tall straight stems and from 5 to 7 flowers are open at one time. It is one of the earliest varieties to bloom, hence valuable as a cut flower sort, either for forcing or outdoor planting.

Per 100, $7.50; per 1000, $65.00. Code Word "Garden."

MARGARET.

A vigorous grower 5 to 6 feet, with broad foliage. The spike is straight and strong. The flowers are large, beautifully arched and arranged in two rows facing the same way, with 6 to 8 open at a time. The color is a brilliant carmine with a large white blotch on lower petals, the white and carmine blending into a violet tint. A good cut flower.

Price—Per 100, $12.00; per 1000, $100.00. Code Word—"Gardenite."

MRS. FRANCIS KING.

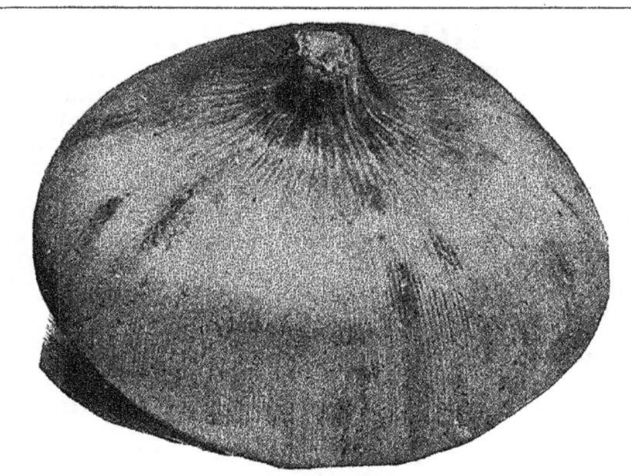

GLADIOLUS GANDAVENSIS. Named Varieties

ALL BULBS LISTED ON THIS PAGE ARE FIRST SIZE.

	TEL. CIPHER.	100.	1000.
Attraction, rich crimson with white throat	Gal	$3.00	$25.00
Augusta, White, blue anthers	Galion	1.75	15.00
Baron J. Hulot, Blue, rich deep indigo shade	Galo	7.00	60.00
Brenchleyensis, Scarlet vermilion	Galon	1.35	11.00
Canary Bird	Galonard	4.50	40.00
Ceres, Pure white, rosy	Galop	1.60	14.00
Eugene Scribe, Large rose	Galopin	4.00	
Jessie, Fine velvety red	Gambado	2.00	18.00
Madam Monneret, Delicate rose	Gamin	2.75	22.50
May, Pure white, flaked rosy crimson	Ganso	3.00	25.00
Shakespeare, White, tinged rose	Garde	4.00	35.00

See our retail catalogue for full list of varieties. Special prices quoted upon application.

GLADIOLUS—Mixtures.

	TEL. CIPHER.	100.	1000.
Scarlet and Red Shades, **Mixed**	Gabarre	$1.25	$10.00
Pink Shades, Mixed	Gabelle	1.50	13.50
Yellow " "	Gabords	3.25	30.00
Scarlet with White Throat	Gaboriou	2.00	18.00
Striped and Variegated, Mixed	Gache	2.50	20.00
Pink and White Mixed, new	Gacone	3.00	23.00
Blue, Mixed	Gadder	5.00	40.00
Good Mixed	Gade	.85	7.00
Seedling Mixture	Gaffe	1.40	12.00
XXX Florists' Mixture, Light and White	Gai	1.50	13.50
Extra Fine Mixed, Light and white, part named	Gaillard	1.85	16.00
Vaughan's "Rainbow" Mixture, made up especially by us from several high-grade mixtures with named sorts added. It is **A 1**	Gain	2.50	22.50
Childsii Mixed, extra large, best selection	Gailant	2.00	17.00

DEALERS' SPECIAL BULB COLLECTION

The Bulbs we offer in this collection we believe are the best suited for counter trade. (Other collections submitted on application.)

250 Gladiolus, good mixed.
250 Gladiolus, extra fine mixed.
50 Caladium, 5-7 inch.
100 Caladium, 7-9 inch.
50 Caladium, 9-11 inch.
50 Begonias, single mixed.
50 Begonias, double mixed.
50 Gloxinias, mixed.
50 Gladiolus, red shades.
50 Gladiolus, pink shades.
50 Gladiolus, striped shades.
50 Gladiolus, yellow shades.
100 Madeira Vines.
500 Tuberoses Dwf. Ex. Pearl I Size.

Price, $25.00.

GREENHOUSE DEPARTMENT.

Note: **On all orders for dormant stock, such as Roses, Hardy Climbers, Shrubs, Fruits and Trees, packing will be charged at cost.**

Besides the few items mentioned below we have Shrubs and Perennials in large quantities in all the popular and best commercial varieties. Ask for our Book for Florists which has a complete list. Special quotations will be made on large orders.

HYDRANGEA PANICULATA GRANDIFLORA.

Our large stock of this is strong, bushy, and has good roots.

	Each.	Dozen.	100.
2 year	$0.20	$2.00	$15.00
2 yr., heavy	.25	2.50	18.00
3 yr.	.30	3.00	22.00
Standards, 1½ to 2 ft. stem	.50	5.00	40.00

OTHELLO PLUM.

The finest purple-leaved ornamental on the market.

	Each.	Dozen.	100.
3 to 4 ft.	$0.40	$4.00	$30.00
4 to 5 ft.	.60	6.00	45.00
5 to 6 ft.	.75	8.00	60.00

PEONIES.

Our own growing, strictly true to name with from 3 to 5 eyes. Ask for complete list. Prices on larger clumps on application.

Unnamed—in separate colors, 3 to 5 eyes.

	Each.	Dozen.	100.
Double Pink, Red, and White	$0.15	$1.50	$10.00
Double Mixed	.10	1.00	6.00

Case Lots.

Specially packed cases, roots one year from division, with 3 to 5 eyes, each with 67 double white, 66 double red, 66 double pink, 200 in all. 200 roots for $18.00; 2 cases for $35.00. We cannot divide cases.

VINES.

Ampelopsis Veitchii—Japan or Boston Ivy.

	Each.	Dozen.	100.
Strong, 2 year	$0.20	$2.00	$12.00
Strong, 3 year	.25	2.50	15.00

Clematis, Large Flowering, Holland Grown.

Beauty of Worcester, sky blue
Henryii, white
Mme. B. Veillard, rose shaded lilac
Gypsy Queen, purple
Jackmani, royal purple
Sieboldi, lavender
Miss Bateman, white
Ville de Lyon, red

	Each.	Dozen.	100.
2 year	$0.30	$3.00	$20.00
3 year	.40	4.20	30.00

Clematis Paniculata, Small Flowering, white.

	Each.	Dozen.	100.
2 year	$0.15	$1.50	$10.00
3 year	.20	2.00	15.00
4 year	.35	3.60	25.00
Kudzu, or Jack and the Beanstalk	.15	1.25	8.00

Matrimony Vine. (Lycium Barbarum.)

	Each.	Dozen.	100.
2 year	$0.15	$1.50	$10.00
3 year	.20	2.00	15.00
4 year	.25	2.50	18.00

DORMANT ROSES.

Not less than 3 of a kind sold at the dozen rate, nor 25 at the 100 rate. Unless noted all are two year, field grown and budded, strong and bushy.

Each, 20c; dozen, $2.00; 100, $14.00.

Alfred Colomb, red
Baroness Rothschild, pink
General Jack, crimson
Mme. G. Luizet, pink
Magna Charta, pink
Mrs. R. G. S. Crawford, flesh
Prince C. de Rohan, crimson
Anna de Diesbach, rose
Baron de Bonstettin, red
Fisher Holmes, crimson
John Hopper, crimson
Mme. Plantier, white
Mrs. John Laing, pink
Paul Neyron, rose
Ulrich Brunner, crimson

DORMANT ROSES—Continued.

Each, 20c; Dozen, $2.00; 100, $15.00.

American Beauty, pink
Caroline Testout, pink
Frau Carl Druschki, white
Gruss an Teplitz, red
J. B. Clark, red
Mabel Morrison, white
Mildred Grant, flesh
Persian Yellow
Captain Christy, flesh
Duchess of Albany
Gloire Lyonaise, yellow
Hermosa, pink
La France, pink
Mme. Abel Chatenay, salmon
M. P. Wilder, red

and many other kinds of H. P. and H. T. Roses.

CLIMBERS.

Each, 30c; Dozen, $3.00; 100, $20.00.

American Pillar, single pink
Hiawatha, single red
White Dorothy Perkins, double.

Each, 25c; Dozen, $2.50; 100, $18.00.

Flower of Fairfield, double red.
Tausendschon, single pink.

	Each.	Dozen.	100.
Crimson Rambler, 2 year	$0.20	$2.00	$15.00
3 year	.25	2.50	18.00
Dorothy Perkins, same as above.			
Excelsa, new, 2 year	.50	4.50	35.00
Lady Gay, 2 year	.25	2.50	18.00
3 year	.25	2.50	16.00
Prairie Queen, 2 year	.20	2.00	15.00
Wichuriana, white, flesh and pink	.20	2.00	15.00

BABY RAMBLERS.

	Each.	Dozen.	100.
Erna Teschendorff, new	$0.50	$5.00	$35.00
Crimson Baby, 2 year	.20	2.00	14.00
3 year	.30	3.00	20.00
Jessie, 2 year	.25	2.50	18.00
3 year	.30	3.00	20.00
Orleans	.30	3.00	20.00
Phyllis, 2 year	.20	2.00	16.00
3 year	.25	2.50	18.00

CANNAS.

We are headquarters. All are leading varieties. Full list on application. For heights, description, etc., see our Book for Florists.

Prices quoted are for both Dormant 1-2 Eyed Bulbs and 3-inch pot plants. Dormant Roots are offered up to April 1 or while stock lasts, after which pot plants are ready.

RED FLOWERING—GREEN FOLIAGE.

	Dormant roots.		3-inch pots.		
	Doz.	100	Each	Doz.	100
Beaute Poitevine, 3½ ft., dark crimson	$0.60	$4.00	$0.10	$0.75	$5.00
Chas. Henderson, 4 ft. Bright crimson	.60	4.00	.10	.75	5.00
Comte de Sach, 4 ft. Clear crimson scarlet	.85	6.00	.15	1.00	7.00
Julius Koch, 3 ft. brilliant blood red	2.00	15.00	.20	2.00	15.00
Milwaukee, 4 ft. Dark maroon	.60	4.00	.10	.85	6.00
New Chicago, 4½ ft. Brilliant scarlet	1.50	10.00	.20	1.50	10.00
Pfitzer's Meteor, 4 ft. Clear orange scarlet	2.00	15.00	.20	2.00	15.00
Prince Wied, 3 ft. Fiery, velvety blood red	1.50	10.00	.15	1.50	10.00
The Express, 2½ ft. Scarlet crimson	5.85	6.00	.15	1.00	8.00

CANNAS—(Continued).

BRONZED LEAVED VARIETIES.

Variety	Dormant roots Doz.	100	3-inch pots Each	Doz.	100
Discolor, 6 ft. Foliage effect only......	.50	3.00	.10	.75	5.00
David Harum, 3½ ft. Vermilion scarlet	.60	4.00	.10	.75	5.00
Director Freudemann, 3½ ft. Scarlet and orange	.60	4.00			
Egandale, 4 ft. Currant red	.60	4.00	.10	.75	5.00
Graf Waldersee, 4 ft. Orange scarlet....	.85	6.00	.15	1.25	8.00
Leonard Vaughan, 4½ ft. Bright scarlet	.60	4.00	.15	.75	5.00
Wm. Saunders, 3½ ft. Deep rich scarlet.	1.25	10.00	.15	1.50	10.00

VARIEGATED RED AND YELLOW SHADES—GREEN FOLIAGE.

Variety	Dormant roots Doz.	100	3-inch pots Each	Doz.	100
Mad. Crozy, 3½ ft. Vermilion with gold border	.60	4.00	.10	.85	6.00
Multiflora, 4 ft. Bright vermilion with yellow border	.60	4.00	.10	.85	6.00
Niagara, 3 ft. Crimson bordered yellow.	.50	3.00			
Queen Charlotte, 4 ft. Orange scarlet with gold band	.60	4.00	.10	.85	6.00
Souv. d'A. Crozy, 4 ft. Crimson with yellow border	.60	4.00	.10	.85	6.00

YELLOW SHADE—GREEN FOLIAGE.

Variety	Dormant roots Doz.	100	3-inch pots Each	Doz.	100
Buttercup, 3½ ft. Clear golden yellow..	.60	4.00	.10	.75	5.00
Dwarf Florence Vaughan, 3 ft. Yellow spotted light crimson	.60	4.00	.10	.85	6.00
Florence Vaughan, 5 ft. Yellow spotted crimson	.60	4.00	.10	.85	6.00

PINK SHADES—GREEN FOLIAGE.

Variety	Dormant roots Doz.	100	3-inch pots Each	Doz.	100
Betsy Ross, 3½ ft. Soft clear pink.....	.60	4.00	.10	.75	5.00

ORCHID FLOWERING CANNAS.

Variety	Dormant roots. Doz.	100	3-inch pots. Each	Doz.	100
Allemania, 4-5 ft. Green foliage, scarlet and yellow	.50	3.00	.10	.75	5.00
Burbank, 5 ft. Green foliage, clear yellow	.50	3.00	.10	.75	5.00
Frederic Benary, 5-6 ft. Green foliage, red, yellow throat and band	.50	3.00	.10	.75	5.00
King Humbert, 4 ft. Bronze foliage, orange scarlet	.75	5.00	.10	.85	6.00
Long Branch, 5 ft. Green foliage, bright crimson bordered yellow............	.85	6.00	.15	1.25	8.00
Louisiana, 6 ft. Green foliage, large vivid scarlet	.60	4.00	.15	.85	6.00
New York, 5 ft. Bronze foliage, rich scarlet	.75	5.00	.15	.85	6.00

WHITE SHADES GREEN FOLIAGE.

Variety	Dormant roots Doz.	100	3-inch pots Each	Doz.	100
Improved Mont Blanc, 3 ft. Pure white..	.85	6.00	.15	1.25	8.00

MIXED CANNAS.

	Dozen	Per 100	Per 1000
Red Shades Green Leaved.........	$0.50	$3.00	$25.00
All Shades Green Leaved..........	.50	3.00	25.00
All Shades Bronze Leaved.........	.50	3.00	25.00

DAHLIAS.

Our Selection of Sorts.

	Divided Field Roots 100	Field Roots 100
Named Red, Pink or Yellow........................	$6.00	$10.00
Named White	8.00	15.00

Double Dahlias, mixed, per 100 field roots, $6.00.

Garden and Farm Tools.

Terms: 1st of Month Following Date of Invoice.
We Do Not Open New Accounts on this Stock Under $25.00.
Please Accompany Order under that amount with Cash.
We Charge Cartage on Orders for Less than Three Machines at a Time.

DRILLS AND SEEDERS.

	EACH LIST PRICE	NET
No. 6 Iron Age Combined Double Wheel Hoe, Hill and Drill Seeder	12.00	9.50
No. 4 Iron Age Combined Double Wheel Hoe and Drill Seeder	$11.00	$ 8.50
No. 4 Iron Age Drill Seeder Attachment	4.00	3.50
No. 6 Iron Age Hill and Drill Seeder Attachment	5.00	4.00
No. 15 Iron Age Combined Single Wheel Hoe, Hill and Drill Seeder	11.00	8.50
No. 17 Iron Age Combined Single Wheel Hoe and Drill Seeder	10.00	8.00
No. 18 Iron Age Drill Seeder	7.50	6.00
No. 8 Iron Age Hill and Drill Seeder	11.00	8.50
No. 22 Iron Age Combined Fertilizer Distributer, Hill and Drill Seeder	18.00	14.00
No. 25 Iron Age Fertilizer Distributor Attachment	4.50	3.60
New Model Drill	8.00	5.90

Cahoon Hand Seeder, each, $2.60; per dozen, $30.00.

CULTIVATORS AND PLOWS.

No. 1 Iron Age Double Wheel Hoe, complete	$ 7.00	$ 5.50
No. 3 Iron Age Double Wheel Hoe, with side hoes only	4.25	3.65
No. 13 Iron Age Double Wheel Hoe, with side hoes and teeth	5.50	4.50
No. 9 Iron Age Single Wheel Hoe, complete	5.25	4.25
No. 12 Iron Age Wheel Hoe, Plow and Cultivator, complete	3.50	3.00
No. 19C Iron Age Wheel Plow and Cultivator	3.50	3.00
No. 20 Iron Age Single Wheel Hoe, complete	6.00	4.70
No. 21 Iron Age Single Wheel Hoe, plain (hoes only)	4.00	3.20
Gem Cultivator, single wheel complete (lots of 6, 10c less)	5.00	4.00
Celery Hiller, Double Mouldboard	16.00	14.00
No. 1 Iron Age Combined Harrow and Cultivator, plain wheel	5.00	4.60
No. 6 Iron Age Horse Hoe and Cultivator, less furrow closing attachment	6.25	5.70

Extras for Iron Age Tools, List Price Less 20 Per cent.

Aprons, Rubber, made of the best quality black sheeting	$1.80	
Barrel Cart, Barrel and Truck with 2½-inch tires	9.50	
" " Truck without barrel, but 1 pair trunnions	7.00	
	EACH	DOZ.
Bellows, American Sulphur, No. 0, small	$0.75	$ 7.50
" " " No. 1, medium	.90	9.50
" " " No. 2, large	1.00	10.50
" Jumbo Powder Guns........Gross, $25.00	.20	2.25
" " " " small .... " 10.50	.10	1.10
" Lowell Dusters	.65	6.75
" Leggett's Little Giant Duster	5.00	

Books, Agricultural; 20 per cent. discount from publishers' prices.
Bone Mills, See Poultry Supplies.

	LB.
Cape Flowers, Pure White. Extra fine quality	$0.90
" " Colored. Bright shades	1.20

Carnation Bands. Tiny rubber bands, almost invisible, per box of 13,000 .... 2.65

" **Supports, Common Sense.** 2-ring, per 100, $1.75; 1000, $15.50; 3-ring, 100, $2.25; 1000 .... 18.00

	Pkg.	12 Pkgs.
Chenille Lettering, silk, all colors	$0.65	$6.50
" " Worsted, large, all colors	.25	2.00
" " " small, " "	.20	1.70
" " Twisted, large, " "	.25	2.00

Clamps, Peerless repair, box of 100, 90c.

Clips, Blake's Lever, per 1000, $1.35.

Corn Planter, the Eagle .... Each 1.10

Dandelion Puller. The "Vaughan," made of malleable iron and unbreakable. A splendid seller. Each, 30c; doz., $3.25; gross, $31.00.

Dibber, Garden, Malleable. Per gross, $28.50; per doz., $3.25; each, 30c

Doves. Vaughan's Flexible. Extra quality, each, $1.15; per doz., $11.50. First quality, each, 95c; doz., $10.50.

FERTILIZERS.

Subject to Market Changes. Terms, Net Cash.

All these fertilizers in bulk are f. o. b. Chicago. If shipped from New York, add 50c per 100 lbs., or $7.00 per ton, except items marked * which are either f. o. b. Chicago or New York. If wanted in 25 or 50 lb. bags, 15c per 100 lbs. extra.

Vaughan's "Rose Grower" Bone Meal, 100 lbs., $2.10; 200 lbs., $3.75; 500 lbs., $8.75; 1,000 lbs., $17.25; 1 ton, $34.00.

Bone Meal, 100 lbs., $1.80; 200 lbs., $3.40; 500 lbs., $8.00; 1,000 lbs., $15.75; ton, $31.00.

Bone Flour, pure white, fine plant food, per 100 lbs., $2.35; 200 lbs., $4.50; 500 lbs., $10.50; 1000 lbs., $20.00; ton, $39.00.

Raw Bone Meal, 100 lbs., $2.10; 200 lbs., $4.00; 500 lbs., $9.50; 1000 lbs., $18.00; ton, $35.00.

Bone Shavings, 100 lbs., $2.60; 200 lbs., $5.00; 500 lbs., $12.00.

Bone and Blood, per 100 lbs., $1.65; 200 lbs., $3.15; 500 lbs., $7.50; 1,000 lbs., $14.50; ton, $28.00.

Bone, Blood and Potash, 100 lbs., $2.40; 200 lbs., $4.60; 500 lbs., $11.00; ton, $41.00.

Cattle Manure, Shredded, 100 lbs., $1.15; 500 lbs., $4.75; 1,000 lbs., $8.00; 2,000 lbs., $14.50.

* Clay's Fertilizer, Imported, 28 lbs., $1.75; 56 lbs., $3.25; 112 lbs., $5.50.

Dried Blood, 100 lbs., $3.50; 200 lbs., $6.90; 500 lbs., $16.75; 1,000 lbs., $33.00.

Fruit and Root Crop Manure, 100 lbs., $1.70; 200 lbs., $3.20; 500 lbs., $7.50; ton, $28.50.

* Peruvian Guano, 100 lbs., $3.00; 200 lbs., $5.50; 1000 lbs., $25.00.

* Horn Shavings, per 100 lbs., $3.75; 500 lbs., $18.25.

Hardwood Ashes, 100 lbs., $1.00; 200 lbs., $1.95; 500 lbs., $4.50; ton, $17.00.

* Ichthemic Guano, 112 lbs., $7.50.

Kainit, per 100 lbs., $1.25; 200 lbs., $2.30; 500 lbs., $5.00; ton, $19.00.

Land Plaster or Gypsum, 100 lbs., 65c; 500 lbs., $2.75.

Muriate of Potash, 100 lbs., $3.00; 200 lbs., $5.75. }
Nitrate of Soda, 100 lbs., $3.50. } Write for prices on larger quantities.

* Scotch Soot, 112 lbs., $3.00.

Sheep Manure, Pulverized, per 100 lbs., $1.10; 500 lbs., $4.85; 1,000 lbs., $8.75; ton, $17.00. Subject to market change.

Sulphate of Potash, 100 lbs., $3.50; 200 lbs., $6.50. (Write for prices on larger lots.)

Sulphate of Ammonia, 100 lbs., $6.00; 500 lbs., $28.50. Write for prices on larger quantities.

* Thompson's Vine and Plant Manure, 112 lbs., $5.00.

* Thompson's Chrysanthemum Manure, 56 lbs, $5.00.

Truck Manure No. 2, "All Soluble," 100 lbs., $1.90; 200 lbs., $3.60; 500 lbs., $8.50; 1,000 lbs., $16.50; ton, $32.50.

Vaughan's High-Grade Truck and Farm Manure, 100 lbs., $2.35; 200 lbs., $4.50; 500 lbs., $10.75; 1,000 lbs., $21.00; ton, $41.00.

* Valsang, 112 lbs., $7.00.

Vaughan's Lawn Fertilizer.

The Best Lawn Dressing on the Market.

Odorless, lasting and effective. A good seller.

	100 lbs.	1000 lbs.
Price, In 5 and 10-lb. packages	$2.90	$28.50
In 25 and 50-lb. bags	2.45	21.50
In 100-lb. bags	2.25	18.50

Fertilizers in Packages for Retailing.

Vaughan's Conc. P. Food, 1-lb. pkgs., box of 2 doz., $3.20. Per doz., $1.75
........½-lb. pkgs., box of 2 doz., $1.80. Per doz., $1.00

Bowker's Plant Food.....1-lb. pkgs., box of 2 doz., $3.80. Per doz., $2.00
" " " ....½-lb. pkgs., box of 2 doz., $2.10. Per doz., $1.10

Flower Gatherer, nickle-plated.......each..$0.80

Flower Seed Gauges. These are made of brass and are very useful in putting up Flower Seeds. Set of 8, per set.......$1.50

Fumigator, Eureka, No. 1, capacity ½ peck.......each.. 1.10
" Eureka, No. 2, capacity 1 peck....... " .. 1.50
" Eureka, No. 3, capacity 2 peeks....... " .. 2.10
" Eureka, No. 4, capacity 3 pecks....... " .. 2.80
" for Nicoticide .... " .. .45

Garden Line, 1000 feet for $4.00; per 100 feet....... .45

Garden Line Reel, per doz., $5.50.......each.. .50

Garden Roller, 2 section, 15 x 16, 150 lbs.
" " 3 section, 15 x 24, 200 lbs.
" " 2 section, 20 x 20, 250 lbs.
" " 2 section, 20 x 24, 300 lbs.
" " 2 section, 24 x 20, 400 lbs.
" " 2 section, 28 x 24, 500 lbs.
" " 3 section, 28 x 30, 600 lbs.

} **Special Prices on Application.**

Glass Cutter, Diamond Universal.......each..$4.00

PERFECTION SIZE 2 SIZE 2½ POINT

PERFECTION GLAZING POINT.

ORIGINAL VAN REYPERS.

On orders for 100,000 and over, we supply cartons, with customer's name on same.

1,000 lots..per 1000.......$0.50
10,000 lots..per 1000....... .45
100,000 lots..per 1000....... .35

Write for prices on larger lots.

Siebert's Improved, ⅝ or ⅞-inch long, lb., 35c; 5 lbs., $1.65; 20 lbs. 6.00

Glazing Tool and Glass Cutter, 3 doz., $1.35.......per doz.. .50

Grafting Wax, ¼ lb., 10c; ½ lb., 18c; lb., 17c; 10 lbs., $1.65. In 25-lb. lots, lb., 15c.

Grass Hooks, English riveted backs, each, 40c.......doz.. 4.25

Grass Collectors:

Philadelphia, Regular 12-inch, $1.50; 14-inch, $1.60; 16-inch, $1.70; 18-inch, $1.80; 20-inch, $1.90....

Philadelphia, for style "K" and High Wheel Mowers, 14 and 15-inch, $1.70; 16-17-inch, $1.80; 18-19-inch, $1.90; 20-21-inch, $2.00.

} **Less 12 per cent Discount.**

Hoes, Scuffle, English, 6-inch, each, 40c; doz., $3.75; 8-inch, each, 50c; doz., $4.50; 10-inch, each, 60c; doz., $5.50.

Hose, "Electric," ¾ inch, 1 to 49 feet, 17½c ft.; 49 to 99 ft., 16½c ft.; 100 to 500 feet, 15½c ft.
" Washers, rubber, for ¾-inch hose.......per gross.. .25
" Clamps, ¾-inch.......dozen, 40c; 3 dozen, $1.10; gross.. 3.75
" Straps, Nos. 4 and 8, doz., 10c; gr., $1.00; No. 12, doz., 12c; gr..1.30

Hose Pliers ....Per doz., $1.50; each.. .15
" Nozzle, Standard, with 2-in. spray, ea., 70c; 2½-in. spray, ea. .85
" Nozzle, Gem......................per dozen, $3.50; each.. .35
" Nozzle, Boston Rose Spray..........................each.. .45
" Nozzle, Bordeaux, ½ inch...........................each.. .60
" Nozzle, Vermorel, ½ inch...........................each.. .60
" Nozzle, Wittbold, ¾ inch...........................each.. .85
" " Chicago, ¾-inch ....each.. 2.25

SNAP HOSE COUPLER.

No. 1

No. 2

No. 3

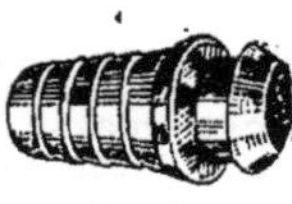
No. 4

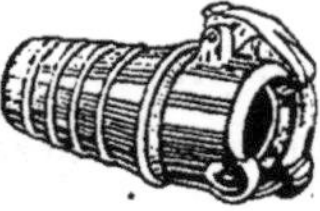
No. 5

Prices for ¾-inch Hose.

No. 1. Screws on to hydrant or old threaded coupling, use with No. 2 or No. 4 in connecting hose. Each, 18c; dozen, $1.75.

No. 2. Screws into faucet or ground pipe, on which it may be left permanently, and to it the hose is attached by the lever connection, No. 1 or No. 5. Can also be screwed into old threaded coupling. Each, 12c; dozen, $1.25.

No. 3. Gooseneck, screws into the old threaded coupling. Most useful at the hydrant. Each, 12c; dozen, $1.10.

No. 4. Corrugated, for insertion directly in the hose. Use with No. 5 for connecting hose. Each, 10c; doz., 85c.

No. 5. Corrugated, for insertion in the hose. Use with No. 4 for connecting hose. Each, 18c; dozen, $2.00.

	Dozen	Gross
Hose Coupler, Brass, ¾-inch..............................	$0.90	$10.60
Hose Mender, Iron, ¾-inch..3 dozen, 80c	.30	
" " Cooper, brass, the best made, ½ and ¾-inch...........	.70	7.50
" " Cooper, brass, 1-inch......	.90	10.00

Hose Reducer, from 1 to ¾ inch...........................each.. .28
Hose Reel, all iron, No. 10..............................each.. 2.15
" " " No. 20..............................each.. 2.35
Hot Bed Mats, Rattan Fibre, 6 feet by 6 feet 2 inches.....each.. 2.25
Hot Bed Mats, Burlap Lined, 40 x 76, each, 85c; doz., $8.50; 76x76, each, $1.35; doz., $13.50.
Hot Bed Mats, Duck, 40x76, each, $1.25; doz., $12.50; 76x76, each, $1.75; doz., $17.50.
Hyacinth Glasses, Packing charges extra.
Tall Belgium, assorted colors. Special prices on application.
Tyes, assorted colors. Special prices on application.
Immortelles, colored, subject to fluctuation,.....per 100 bunches.. 28.50
" natural, subject to fluctuation.....per 100 bunches.. 21.00

INSECT DESTROYERS. Write for prices on large lots.

Ant Exterminator. A non-poisonous powder. Small box, 10c; larger box .... .20
Arsenate of Lead, 1-lb. tins, 16c; 5-lb. tin, 75c; 25-lb. keg, $3.25; 100-lb. keg $11.00
Aphine, 1 pt., 50c; 1 quart, 90c; 1 gallon.................. 2.25
Aphis Punk, 1 pkg., 12 sheets, 55c; per case, 144 sheets...... 6.00
Bordeaux Mixture, liquid, 1-quart cans, 35c each; dozen, $3.70; case (36), $10.40; 1 gallon, 80c; case (12), $8.75; 5-gallon can, $3.50; case (2)................................ 6.00
Bordeaux Mixture, powder, 1-lb. cartons, ea., 20c; doz., $2.20; 100 for $17.00; 28-lb. keg............................ 4.50
Eureka Weed Killer, 3-lb. tins, each, 75c; doz., $8.50; 12 lb. tin, $2.50; doz. 25.00
Fir Tree Oil Soap, ½-lb. tins, each, 23c; doz., $2.50; 2-lb. tins, 65c each.

INSECT DESTOYERS—Continued.

Item	Price
Flowers of Sulphur (subject to fluctuation), 10 lbs., 40c; (bbl. lots, 3¼c lb.); 100 lbs	3.40
Fish Oil Soap, 1-lb. cartons, each, 13c; 25 for $3.00; 50 for $5.50; ½-lb. cartons; each, 7c; 25 for $1.65; 50 for	3.25
Grape Dust, Hammond's, 5-lb. packages, 30c; per 100 lbs., bulk	4.50
Hellebore, Powdered, 1-lb. pkgs., 27c each; case lots, 50 1-lb. packages	12.00
Horicum, New Scale Remedy, per gal., 90c; 5 gals	4.00
Kerosene Emulsion, 1-qt. cans, each, 35c; per doz., $3.85; case (36), $11.00; gal. tin, 85c; case (12), $9.60; 5 gals., $3.25 case (2)	6.00
Lime Sulphur Solution, 1-quart cans, ea., 28c; doz., $3.25; case (36), $9.00; 1 gal., 65c; case (12), $7.25; 5 gal. $2.50; case (2)	4.50
Lemon Oil, in tins, ½-pt. tin, 20c ea.; pint, ea., 35c; per quart, 60c; ½ gal., $1.00; per gal., $1.70; 5 gal	8.00
Nicoticide, 1 pint, $2.25; ½ pint, $1.15; 4 ounces, 65c; quart, $4.25; ½ gallon, $7.25; gallon	13.50
Nikoteen, 4 oz. bottle, 35c each; case of 48 bottles, $15.00; ½ pint, 70c; case of 10 bottles, $6.50; per pint, $1.35; case, 10 pints	12.00
Nico-Fume, best and cheapest fumigating material, per tin 24 sheets, 65c; 144 sheets, $3.25; 288 sheets	5.85
Nico-Fume, Liquid, ¼ pt., 45c; 1 pt., $1.35; ½ gal., $5.00; gal.	9.75
Paris Green (write for market price).	
Persian Insect Powder, 10 lbs., $3.25; lb., 35c; ½ lb	.20
Slug Shot, in bulk, in bbl., lots f. o. b. cars.......per 100 lbs.	4.00
" " 1-lb. cartons, each, 15c; doz., $1.60; case, 48, $5.20; gross	12.20
" " 5-lb. pkgs., ea., 30c; bbl. lots, f. o. b. cars, 100 lbs.	4.35
Slug Shot Dusters, gal. size.......Each,	.30
Solution of Copper, pint, 35c; quart, 55c; gal	1.60
Scalecide, qt., 50c; gallon, $1.10; 5 gallons	4.75
Thrip Juice, per pint	.55
Tobakine, ¼ pint, 60c; ½ pint, $1.10; pint, $2.00; ½ gallon, $7.75; gallon	15.00
Tobacco Soap, Sulpho, in ½-lb. pkgs., each, 15c; per doz., $1.60; 3 dozen	4.50
Tobacco Soap, Sulpho, in 2-oz. pkgs., each, 8c; per doz	.80
" Dust. fine black stuff, per 100 lbs	3.25
" " regular grade, 1000 lbs., $14.00; per 100 lbs.	1.65
" " fumigating kind, 100 lbs	3.25
" Stems, only in full bales of about 150 lbs., per 100 lbs., $1.25; per 1000 lbs., $9.00 (3 bales and over at 1000-lb. rate).	
Wilson's Plant Oil, pt., 35c; qt., 65c; gal	1.65
X. L. All liquid insecticide, per ½ gal., $2.00; per gal	3.75

KNIVES.

	EACH.	DOZ.
Asparagus.—American	$0.25	$2.75
Budding (715B).—Imported, black handle, ivory tip	.80	9.00
English (716I).—Ivory handle	1.10	12.50
Saynor—No. 400	1.15	13.50
Beech handle (302½), with Stationary blade	.20	2.25
Propagating (713I).—English, ivory handle	1.10	12.50
Vaughan's Florist	.60	6.25
Two-bladed, stag handle with pruning and budding blade	1.15	12.50
Saynor—No. 401	1.10	13.00
Putty Knife.—No. 120, a very good tool	.20	2.50
Potato.—Humphrey's Concave, per gross, $15.00		1.85
Flower Seed Counting Knife.—Very handy for counting seed and dividing up small quantities of fine and expensive seeds	.20	

Land Plaster.—See Fertilizers.

Philadelphia Lawn Mowers.

TERMS: NET CASH.

High Wheel (Steel), Style A.

It has 10-inch driving wheels, 6½-inch cylinder cutters with four knives.

Width	Weight	List Price	
15-inch	40 lbs.	$25.00	Discount 60 and 10 per cent.
17-inch	42 lbs.	28.00	
19-inch	44 lbs.	31.00	
21-inch	46 lbs.	34.00	

Style K.—10-inch, high wheel, 5 knife open wiper with patent corrugated blades.

Width	Weight	List Price	
14-inch	40 lbs.	$20.00	Discount 70 and 10 per cent.
16-inch	42 lbs.	22.00	
18-inch	44 lbs.	24.00	
20-inch	46 lbs.	26.00	

The Vaughan Mower.

Specially manufactured for our sale, high wheel, four-blade mower.

Width	Net Price	Width	Net Price
15-in.	$7.25	19-in.	$10.00
17-in.	8.00	21-in.	10.50

Crestlawn Mower.
Strongest, easiest running mower built. Eleven-inch Ball Bearing drive wheels and automatic interlocking frame that cannot be knocked out of adjustment.

	List Price	Net
14-in.	$12.00	$ 8.50
16-in.	13.00	9.50
18-in.	14.00	11.00
20-in.	15.00	11.50

Victory Ball Bearing.

The best and smoothest running ball bearing mower on the market.

Width	Net Price	Width	Net Price
14-in.	$8.00	20-in.	$10.15
16-in.	9.25	22-in.	10.35
18-in.	9.85	24-in.	11.25

Lawn Sweeper, The Gem.
Best Lawn Sweeper on the market. Each, $14.00.

Lawn Horse Boots, The Link. Made in 3 sizes.
No. 2 for No. 2 horse shoe, 5½ in. inside measure.
No. 4 for No. 4 horse shoe 6½ in. inside measure.
No. 6 for No. 6 horse shoe 7 in. inside measure.
Per set of 4, $8.00.

POT AND TREE LABELS.

We carry the best quality of Wooden Labels made in the country; they are smooth, strong and neat. Samples free.

In lots of 5000 we allow a discount of 5%.

Item		Per 1000 Plain	Per 1000 Painted
Pot Labels, Wooden, 4-inch, plain	10,000, $4.50	$0.50	
" " " 4-inch, painted	10,000, 5.65		$0.65
" " " 5-inch		.70	.85
" 6-inch		.80	1.10
" 8-inch		1.50	2.50
" 10-inch		2.75	4.00
" 12-inch		5.00	5.50
Tree Labels, Wooden, 3½-inch, notched		.55	.75
" " " 3½-inch, iron wired		.70	.90
" " " 3½-inch, copper wired		.90	1.10
Copper Labels, wired, indestructible...No. 1, per 100, .90			
" " " " ...No. 2, per 100, 1.30			
Aluminum Tree Labels	per 100, 1.75		15.00
Leaf Mould, for Ferns, etc.	per bbl.		1.50

Mastica, for glazing. 22 gals., $23.50; 10 gals., $11.30; 6 gals., $7.20; per gal. 1.25
" **Machine**, 5 for $5.50 .... each 1.15

Match Sticks, per 1000, 5-inch, 40c; 12-inch, 75c; 18-inch, $1.00.
Packages contain 250 sticks. We do not break packages.

MATTING, Porto Rico. Used by all leading florists for decorating Azaleas, Hyacinths, Tulips, and in fact all blooming plants. They increase the sales of blooming plants.

Solid Colors, each, 16c ..... per doz.. 1.65

Plain, Fancy Striped and Figured, each, 20c ..... " " .. 2.25

MOLE TRAPS,
Out o'Sight ..... each.. .70

MOSS. (See also Sphagnum.)
French green, in square packages, pkg., 8c; per doz., 70c; per 100 ..... 4.75

Sheet Moss. Per sack 1.35

Moss Wreaths. Bright green, good sellers, 10-inch, doz., $1.15; 100, $9.00; 12-inch, doz., $1.35; 100, $10.50; 14-inch, doz., $1.55; 100 ..... 12.00

Mount Beacon Green, for shading greenhouses, gal., $1.55; 5 gals... 7.50

PAMPAS PLUMES. Natural. 24 to 36 inches. Per 1000, $23.50; per 100 ..... 2.75

Paper, Manilla Wax, light, per 400 sheets 1.30
" " Tissue, 10 reams, $4.85; (400 sheets) ..... .50
" Florists' White Tissue, per 4,000 sheets, $9.50; (400 sheets).. 1.00
" American Beauty Tissue, per ream, 55c; 10 reams 5.00
" White Wax (400 sheets) 1.50
" Green Wax (400 sheets) 1.75
" Waterproof Crepe, per dozen rolls 2.25

Peat, Azalea, per bbl., F. O. B. Chicago 1.80
" **for Orchids (fern roots), per bbl** 1.90

Pencils, Indelible, per dozen, 90c ..... each.. .10

Pins, Florists'. Glass heads, in black and white. Boxes of 1000.

1-inch	1½-inch	2-inch	2½-inch	3-inch	3½-inch	4-inch
45c	70c	90c	$1.10	$1.35	$1.55	$1.70

Plant Bed Cloth. Patent, per yard, medium, 9c; heavy, 14c.
We do not sell less than 20 yards of a kind.

CANE STAKES.

Standard Grade. From 6 to 8 feet long; weight, about 175 lbs. per 1000.
Price (if shipped from Chicago), per 100, 70c; 250 for $1.35; per 1000, $4.80.
Price (if shipped New York), per 100, $1.15; 250 for $2.50; per 1,000, $6.50.
Special price on larger lots on application.

Extra Heavy Grade. For special work, Dahlias, etc. These run from 9 to 12 feet in length and weigh about 360 pounds per 1000.
Price (in Chicago only), per 100, $1.45; 250 for $3.25; 1000, $12.00.

Pipe Stems. For light work; 4 to 6 ft.
Price (from Chicago only), per 100, 50c; 250 for $1.00; 1000 for $3.00.

Japanese Bamboo Canes, light, strong and durable, per 100, 60c; 250 for $1.35; 1000 for $5.00; 5000 for $23.75.

Green Painted Japanese Bamboo. 2-ft., per 100, 35c; per 1000, $3.15; 2½-ft., per 100, 50c; per 1000, $4.25; 3-ft., per 100, 60c; per 1000, $5.40; 4-ft., per 100, 70c; per 1000, $6.25.

Plant Stakes, Wooden, Light turned, painted green, per 100, 18-inch, 80c; 2-ft., $1.55; 2½-ft., $2.35; 3-ft., $3.25; 3½-ft., $4.00; 4-ft., $5.00; 5-ft., $5.75. Heavy, per 100, 3-ft., $4.90; 4-ft., $6.25; 5 ft., $8.00.

Plant Stakes, Galvanized Steel Wire. Terms, net cash.
Price subject to advance without notice.

NO. 9 WIRE	PER 100	PER 1000
1½-foot	$0.30	$2.50
2 "	.40	3.50
2½ "	.50	4.50
3 "	.65	5.50

NO. 8 WIRE	PER 100	PER 1000
3½-foot	$0.80	$7.25
4 "	1.00	8.75
5 "	1.25	10.35

Plant Stand. Rolling Fiber.

	EACH	DOZ.		EACH	DOZ.
12-inch	$0.65	$5.50	18-inch	$1.00	$ 9.75
14 "	.75	6.75	20 "	1.20	11.40
16 "	.95	8.35	22 "	1.55	14.00

Pots. Neponset Flower. We are Sole Western Agents. F. O. B. Chicago, less 5 per cent in New York.

2¼-inch, packed 1000 to crate, per 100, 25c; per 1000, $2.15
2½-inch, packed 1000 to crate, per 100, 30c; per 1000, $2.50
3-inch, packed 1000 to crate, per 100, 40c; per 1000, $3.40.
3½-in., packed 1000 to crate, per 100, 55c; per 1000, $4.85.
4-inch, packed 500 to crate, per 100, 75c; per 1000, $6.00.
5-inch, packed 500 to crate, per 100, $1.15; per 1000, $9.75.
6-inch, packed 500 to crate, per 100, $1.55; per 1000, $13.70.

Pot Hangers, Kramer's....................per doz..$1.00

FLOWER POTS, WHITE EARTHEN F. O. B. Chicago only.

	100	1000		100	1000
2 inch	$0.40	$3.50	5 inch	$1.60	$14.00
2½ inch	.50	4.00	6 "	2.50	23.00
3 "	.60	5.25	7 "	4.50	
3½ "	.70	6.00	8 "	7.00	
4 "	.90	8.10	9 "	9.00	
4½ "	.95	8.75	10 "	14.50	
			12 "	22.00	

BULB OR FERN PANS.	DOZ.	100	SAUCERS.	100
5 inch	$0.25	$ 1.85	4 inch	$ 0.90
6 "	.35	2.85	5 "	1.15
7 "	.65	4.50	6 "	1.60
8 "	.80	6.15	7 "	2.00
10 "	1.40	12.80	8 "	2.60
12	1.90	18.00	9 "	3.60
			10 "	4.50
			12 "	7.25

RED FLOWER POTS.

Sold in crates only. F. O. B. Chicago.

	No. Pots in Crate.				No. Pots in Crate.	
2 inch	1500	$3.60 per 1000		6 inch	100	$ 3.15 per 100
2½ "	1000	5.00 " "		7 "	75	4.80 " "
3 "	500	7.90 " "		8 "	50	7.25 " "
4 "	250	1.10 per 100		10 "	12	16.50 " "
5 "	200	1.90 " "		12 "	10	30.00 " "

PUMPS.

Success Spray Pump, best bucket pump made.......... 3.50
Sunshine Spray Pump, for orchard work complete with 2 leads hose.......... 8.25
Iron Age Vertical Barrel Spray Pump No. 191, without barrel..........12.50
Iron Age, 50 gal. horizontal, with single acting pump....17.50
Bordeaux Spray Nozzles, each 60c.; doz.......... 6.50
Vermorel Nozzle, each, 60c; doz.......... 6.50
The Kinney, each.......... 1.75
Putty, Twemlow's Old English, semi-liquid, for glazing, in 1, 2 and 3 gal. kits, per gallon, $1.50; 5 and 10 gal. kits, per gal.......... 1.45
Putty Bulb, Scollays, each, 75c; doz.......... 8.60

RAPHIA, NATURAL—Regular grade.
Prices subject to change.

	F.O.B.CHICAGO. Per lb.	F.O.B.N.Y. Per lb.
5 lb. lots	$0.15	$0.15
10 lb. lots	.13	.13
25 lb. lots to 50 lbs	.12	.11½
100 lb. lots	.10½	.10
Bale lots, about 225 lbs	.08	.07½

RAPHIA NATURAL—Florist grade.

	F. O. B. CHICAGO. Per lb.	F. O. B. N. Y. Per lb.
5 lb. lots	$0.18	$0.18
10 lb. lots	.16	.16
25 to 50 lb. lots	.15	.14½
100 lb. lots	.12½	.12
Bale lots, about 225 lbs	.09	.08½

RAPHIA, COLORED.

	Per lb.
1 lb. lots	$0.35
5 lb. lots	.33
25 lb. lots	.30
50 lb. lots	.27
100 lb. lots	.25

TERMS: First of month following date of invoice.
We do not open new accounts on this stock under $25.00.
Please accompany order under that amount with cash.

REEDS.

	Per lb. in 1 lb. lots.	Per lb. in 5 lb. lots
No. 1	$0.50	$0.48
No. 2	.45	.40
No. 3	.40	.38
No. 4	.38	.36
No. 5	.36	.33
No. 6	.33	.31
No. 8	.25	.21

	Per oz.	¼ lb.	Per lb.	5 lbs.
Splints	$0.10	$0.30	$1.15	$4.50
Sweet Grass	.10	.25	.85	
Wood Ribbon	.08	.25	.90	4.00

If desired we can put the above up in packages to retail at 10 cents each, the cost to you being 5 cents each if ordered in dozen lots or more.

BOOKS ON BASKET MAKING, ETC.

Indian Basketry.—By James. Cloth, 402 pages. Illustrated....... $2.25
Raphia and Reed Weaving.—By E. S. Knapp. Cloth, 182 pages. Fine for school work. Illustrated.... .45
Basket Making.—By T. Vernette Morse. Paper, 32 pages. Richly illustrated. Fine for beginners .... .20
How to Make Baskets.—This is the title of a very instructive work by Mary White. Bound in cloth, 194 pages. Illustrated. Price.... $0.90
More Baskets and How to Make Them, by Mary White.... .90

Rake, Automatic, self-cleaning, 26 wood teeth.... each.. .60
English Daisy, 20 teeth.... 2.50
Lawn Queen, 24 wire teeth, reversible head, 30c; Jumbo, 36 teeth. .60
Steel Bow, garden. Does not break in the center; 12 teeth, 50c; 14 teeth, 65c; 16 teeth.... .70

Rustic Hanging Baskets.	9 inch.	11 inch.	12 inch.	14 inch
Each	$0.75	$1.00	$1.18	$1.65

Sash, Hot Bed. No. 1 Norway Pine, 3x6 feet, unglazed, doz., $16.25; 3 ft. 2 in. by 6 ft., unglazed, doz.... 17.50
Saw, Pruning, double edge, 16-in., each, 70c; dozen.... 8.00
18-in., each, 80c; doz., $9.00; 20-in., each, 90c; doz. 9.85
Vaughan's Perfection. With adjustable blade, suitable for hand and pole saw, each, $1.25; doz., $14.50. Extra blades, each .... .20

Scythe Blades. English; 30 inch, each, $1.10; 36 inch, $1.20; 40 inch 1.25
" **Snath** .... .80
" Stones. Talacre, imported, each, 15c; per dozen........... 1.50

SEED BAGS. We furnish 250 and over of a size at the 1000 rate, smaller quantities are billed at an advance of 15 per cent. over 1000 rate.
These prices do not include printing.

Per 1000

Miniature, 2½x⅞ inches for Flower Seed, 5000 for $3.50......$0.75
Yellow, 2⅜x3⅝ inches (No. 656), for Flower Seed, not gummed .90
Yellow, 1 oz., per 1000, $1.00; 2 oz........................... 1.20
White, 2x3⅝ inches (No. 1530B), for Flower Seed, gummed; 5000 for $3.00... .65
Extra Heavy, per 1000, 1 oz., $1.00; 2 oz., $1.20; 4 oz., $1.50; ½ pint, $1.80; 1 pint, $2.50; quart, $2.75; 3 pints, $3.75; 2 quarts, $4.25; 3 quarts, $5.25; 4 quarts, $7.75; 6 quarts, $9.50; 8 quarts.. 11.25

Seed Gauges, for Flower Seeds, brass, set of 8, per set............. 1.50
" " for Vegetable Seeds, tin, set of 4, per set............. 1.00

SHEARS.

German Pruning.—Improved Spring, 4½-inch, doz., $8.00; each, 80c; 5½-inch, per doz., $9.75; each, 90c; 6½-inch, per doz., $10.50; each, $1.00; 7½-inch, per doz., $11.25; each, $1.05; 8½-inch, per doz., $12.85; each, $1.15; 9½-inch, per doz., $14.50; each, $1.30; extra springs for same, doz., 85c; 10c each.
Buckeye Pruning ....each..$1.00
Clyde Draw Cut, long handle.......................each.. 1.85
Sheep, with thumb guard, each, 30c.................per doz.. 3.50
Improved Wire-Cutting, for Florist, per doz., $7.80.....each.. .70
Border English, long handles, 9-inch blade, each, $1.75, with wheel... 2.00
Grass, English, long handles with 2 wheels, 9-inch........... 2.15
Hedge, English, 8-inch blade, 90c; 9-inch, $1.20; 10-inch...... 1.40
" " notched, 8-inch, $1.00; 9-inch, $1.25; 10-inch. 1.50

Sod Cutter, Richmond ....each..21.00
SOD CRUSHER NO. 1 MACHINE, total height, 3½ feet; height of box, 18 inches; width, 20 inches; length, 24 inches. Price in New York, $13.50; in Chicago, $14.00. No. 2 Machine, $18.00.
Sphagnum Moss. Burlap bales, each, $1.65; 10 for $15.00.
Write for prices on larger lots.
" " Wired bales, each, $1.00; 10 for $9.00.

SPRAYERS.

Each

Auto Spray, galvanized tank, stop cock......$3.75
Auto Spray, galvanized tank and auto pop... 4.25
Auto Spray, brass tank and stop cock.each.. 5.10
Auto Spray, brass tank and auto pop........ 5.75
Auto Spray Hand Pump, galvanized, qt. size, 65c each; brass...................... 1.15
The Brandt, Galvanized, Steel Tank..each.. 4.35
The Brandt, brass tank, each.............. 5.50
The Lowell, glass tank, all tin, doz., $6.50... .60
Simplex Spray Pump, brass, 3½ gallon, complete, $6.75; galvanized, complete. 4.00
Brass extension rod, 24 in. long....... .30
Pneumatic. galvanized, 90c; brass......... 1.35

SPRINKLERS.

Merrill's Rotary or Butterfly, each, 25c; per doz. 2.75
Evanston, each, 30c..........per doz.. 3.25

BRANDT SPRAYER.

Hartford, 2 foot, each, 65c; doz., $6.50; 4 foot, each, 75c; per doz.. 7.80

SPRINKLERS—Continued

Scollay's Rubber.

None better for floral work. Beware of cheap imitations. We are sole Chicago Agents.

	Each.	Dozen.
Large size, No. 1..	$0.70	$7.75
Medium size, No. 3	.45	5.90
Small size, No. 4..	.40	4.25
Angle Neck, large size, No. 1......	.70	8.00

The Lenox. Good seller; dozen.$3.50

SYRINGES

American, Brass, B, $2.15; C, $3.25; D, $3.80; No. 5, $5.50; No. 0 ....$1.75
No. 12, English, Brass, with two sprays and 1 stream, 14-inch.. 2.50
No. 11, 18-inch, same style and size as No. 5............each.. 3.75
Thermometer, Common, tin case, 8-inch, 3 dozen, $3.25..per doz.. 1.15
" " " " 10-inch, 3 " 4.00.. " " .. 1.40
" Cabinet, wood case, metal face........... " " .. 3.50
" Self-Registering, 8-inch tin case.............each.. 2.50
" Hot-bed, wooden frame.....................each.. 1.70
" Imported German, all glass.................each.. .25
" Minimum. For registering cold during absence and showing present temperature...........each.. 1.50
Thistle Cutter, per dozen, $4.00...........................each.. 0.40
Tin Foil, 5 or 7-inch, per 100 lbs. (net cash), subject to change.... 8.00
Tooth Picks, per case of 100 boxes, including cartage (net cash).. 4.75
" " Wired, per box of 10,000, $1.60; 5 boxes for........ 7.00

Tobacco Stems. See "Insecticides."

Tomato Supports, heavy galvanized wire, per doz., $1.60; per gross 18.00
Tree Pruner, Waters', each, 4-foot pole, 50c; 6-foot pole.......... .60
" " 8-foot pole, 70c; 10-foot pole, 80c; 12-foot pole...... .90
" " extra blades, dozen, $1.25...................each.. .12

TERMS. First of month following date of invoice. We do not open new accounts on this stock under $25.00.
Please accompany order under that amount with cash.

Trellises, Fan, per dozen, 18-inch, $1.25; 24-inch, $2.00; 30-inch, $3.00; 36-in., $3.50; 3½-foot, $4.25; 4-foot, $5.50; 5-foot, $7.00; 6-foot, $8.00; 7-foot.............................. 9.25
Veranda, per dozen, 5-foot, $6.75; 6-foot, $8.00; 7-foot, $10,00; 8-foot, $11.50; 9-foot, $14.50; 10-foot.................. 16.00
Trowels, Vaughan's Steel, the best, per dozen, $5.00........each.. .45
Trowels, Garden, per dozen lots, 6-inch, 65c..............gross.. 7.00
" English Steel, 6-inch, each, 18c; per dozen, $2.00..gross.. 17.50

COLUMBIAN PLANT TUBS.

	F. O. B. Chicago Each	4 for
11 x 11½ inches	$0.75	$2.80
14 x 14½ "	1.20	4.40
17 x 16½ "	1.60	6.00
19 x 19¾ "	2.00	7.40
20¾ x 22½ "	2.25	8.40

UNION CYPRESS FLOWER TUBS.

An excellent tub, cheap, neat and durable. Made from ⅞-inch cypress, with iron handles and wooden feet, three iron hoops and two coats of green paint.

	DIAMETER.	HEIGHT.	Each	4 for
No. 1.	11½ inches	11½ inches	$0.80	$3.00
No. 2.	13½ "	11¼ "	1.00	3.80
No. 3.	14¾ "	14 "	1.40	5.25
No. 4.	16 "	15 "	1.80	6.75
No. 5.	19 "	18 "	2.40	9.25
No. 6.	22 "	19½ "	3.25	12.00

Write for Discounts on Larger Lots.

Turf Edger, round edge, per dozen, $5.00; 3 for $1.30........each..$0.45
" " English half moon, without handle, dozen, $9.75; each.. .90

TWEEZERS for Florists.—Imported.
4-inch, each, 8c; per dozen...$0.85 6-inch, each, 15c; per dozen..$1.40
5-inch, each, 12c; per dozen... 1.35

TWINE.

"The Queen" White Cotton. For tying parcels, flowers, etc. Put up in 5-lb. sacks. Price.................................... 1.40

Hemp. No. 18. For parcels, per lb.............................. .28

Linen, Red and white; best for training Smilax (4 balls to lb.), 3-lb. pkg., $1.20; per lb.. .45
Green, for packages, very strong. Per lb.................. .50

Jute. For bunching, 2 or 3-ply; per lb., 15c; 10 lbs., $1.40; 100 lbs. 12.00
For bunching, 1-ply, runs twice as far as any other. Per lb., 16c; 10 lbs., $1.50; 100 lbs............................ 13.00

Silkaline. For stringing Smilax, etc.; fast green colors, will not fade or break.
FFF, Coarse, 2-oz. spools, 1-lb. in box, 8 spools.............. 1.15
FF, Medium, " " " " " 1.15
F, Fine, " " " " " 1.15

Florists' Thread. Similar to Silkaline. Samples on application.
"King Arthur" brand, 2-oz. spools, 10c each..........dozen .90

Florists' Glazed Fibre Vases. Indurated Fibre Florists' Vases for cut-flower displays and storage purposes cannot be excelled for richness, beauty and economy. They are too well-known to the Florist trade to require extended comment

No.	Depth	Diameter	Each	Doz.
No. 1.	Depth, 10 inches	diameter, 5½ inches	$0.40	$4.50
" 2.	" 9 "	" 4½ "	.35	4.00
" 3.	" 6 "	" 4 "	.35	3.50
" 4.	" 4½ "	" 3 "	.25	2.60
" 11.	" 18 "	" 5½ "	.50	5.35
" 22.	" 15 "	" 4½ "	.40	4.60
" 33.	" 12 "	" 4 "	.40	4.00
" 0.	" 13 "	" 8 "	.50	5.35
" 00.	" 22 "	" 9 "	1.85	19.50
" 000.	" 29 "	" 9 "	2.50	25.00
" 01.	" 20 "	" 7 "	1.00	11.50

Vases. Green Earthenware.

No.	Diameter	Depth	Each	Doz.
No. 1.	Diameter, 4 inches	depth, 12 inches	$0.25	$2.75
" 2.	" 5½ "	" 10 "	.30	3.25
" 3.	" 4½ "	" 15 "	.35	3.75
" 4.	" 5½ "	" 18 "	.60	6.75

Vase, Clara Cemetery, each, 20c; doz., $2.25; per barrel of 3 doz. $5.60.

Watering Pots, American, galvanized iron, long spout, round, 2 copper faced roses with each pot. 4 quarts, each, $1.60; 6 quarts, each, $1.70; 8 quarts, each, $1.90; 10 quarts, each, $2.25; 12 qts. 2.50

French (oval) style, same make; 6 quarts, $2.00; 8 quarts, $2.25; 10 quarts, $2.50; 12 quarts 2.75

Wheelbarrow, The Vaughan Greenhouse 4.00

" The Globe Garden 3.75

WEEDERS.

Combination, per gross, $19.50	per dozen	1.75
Lang's, per gross, $15.00	"	1.50
Excelsior, per gross, $5.75	"	.65
Hazeltine, per gross, $19.00	"	1.75
Eureka, short handled, per doz., $2.50; long handled	"	3.00
B's Weed Extractor, with step	"	4.25
Piqua Lawn Weeder, each, 70c	"	8.00
Magic Weeder and Hoe, each, 30c	"	3.50

EUREKA WEEDER.

COMBINATION WEEDER.

LANG'S WEEDER.

HAZELTINE WEEDER.

MAGIC WEEDER AND HOE.

EXCELSIOR WEEDER.

FLORISTS' CUT WIRE.

In Wooden Boxes.

The wire is prepared especially for Florists. Is clean, extra soft, white wire, straightened and cut in lengths ready for immediate use, and in a convenient form. 12 lbs. in each box, in lengths of 12 or 18 inches.

No. 20	22	24	26	28	30	36
$0.90	$1.10	$1.20	$1.50	$1.85	$2.05	$2.75

BRIGHT ANNEALED WIRE.

Prices subject to change.

	12 lbs.		12 lbs.
No. 18	$0.55	No. 26	$0.85
No. 20	.60	No. 27	.90
No. 22	.70	No. 28	.95
No. 24	.75	No. 36	1.75

TRADE LIST OF

POULTRY SUPPLIES.

TERMS NET CASH.

We carry a complete line and shall be pleased to hear from you when in want of anything in this line. We fill orders promptly and make prices as low as possible. We quote here some leading articles, description of these and other goods given fully in retail list. Write for prices on items not listed here. Prices, F. O. B., Chicago, except where noted.

BONE CUTTERS.

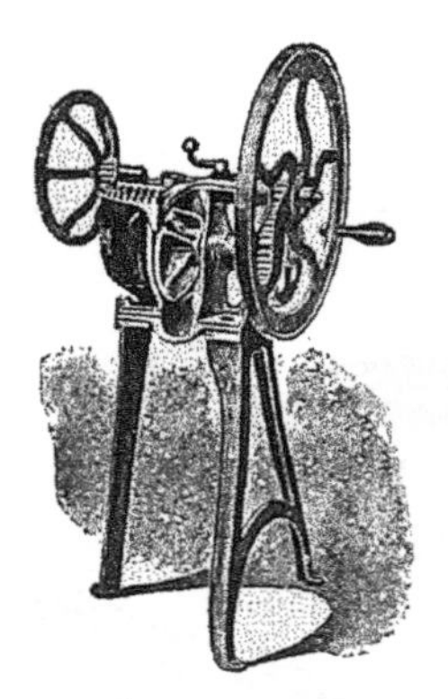

NO. 1 HUMPHREY.

The Humphrey.—Simple, large capacity, easy to operate. The only open hopper green bone cutter that is also a practical vegetable cutter.

	Retail	Net.
No. 1. Hand power	$12.00	$10.75
No. 2. Small power	13.50	12.10
No. 2½ Hand and power	15.00	13.50

Mann's Bone Cutter.—Standard, popular and well-known.

	Retail	Net.
No. 7, with balance wheel and iron stand. Patented 1902. Model automatic governing spring feed. Large open-hinged cylinder. Intended for flocks of from 50 to 200 fowls	$12.00	$10.75
Wilson's "Crown" Bone cutter without stand	6.50	6.00
Wilson's "Crown" Bone Cutter with stand	8.00	7.80
No. 1. Bone Mill for crushing dry bones, shells, etc., without stand	5.00	4.50
No. 1. Bone mill with stand	7.00	6.00

Wilson's Family Grist Mill for grinding and crushing all kinds of grains.

	Retail	Net.
No. 0. Family Grist Mill without stand	5.00	4.50

Humphrey's Rapid Clover Cutter.—Forty cuts of the knife to each revolution of hand wheel; easily operated.

	Retail	Net.
Rapid Clover cutter with stand	10.50	9.50

NO. 0 FAMILY GRIST MILL.

WHITEWASH AND SPRAY PUMPS.

The 0-2 Whitewash Sprayer	ret. $6.50 .. net.	$5.40
"Success" Bucket Sprayer, is double acting, throwing continuous spray		3.50
The Lowell, glass tank, all tin, each 60c	doz.	6.50
Tennant, large size, each, 65c	doz.	7.00
" medium size, each 50c	doz.	5.50
" small size, each 35c	doz.	4.00

PRAIRIE STATE INCUBATORS AND BROODERS.

The Prairie State is the safest and most reliable Incubator a merchant can sell; every machine is guaranteed by the manufacturer and no risk whatever is assumed by the purchaser.

The Prairie State, because of its system of regulation and ventilation, is the most easily operated and the most certain in results of all incubators. It has done more to make poultry-raising profitable than all other machines combined. It is a machine upon which you can depend. It is the machine you want.

They have the best regulator ever placed in an incubator—the only thermostat which takes the temperature from both the upper and lower sides of the egg tray, thus controlling the heat in all parts of the egg chamber.

PRICE LIST OF INCUBATORS.

	Retail.	Net.
No. 0.—Diffusion, 100 hen eggs, 87 lbs. net weight; 135 lbs. crated	$18.00	$16.20
No. 1.—Diffusion, 150 hen eggs, 115 duck eggs—108 lbs. net weight; 160 lbs. crated	22.50	20.25
No. 2.—Diffusion, 240 hen eggs, 200 duck eggs—175 lbs. net weight; 240 lbs. crated	32.00	28.80
No. 3.—Diffusion, 390 hen eggs, 300 duck eggs—220 lbs. net weight; 275 lbs. crated	38.00	34.20
No. 2.—Junior, 115 hen eggs, 70 lbs. net weight, 95 lbs. crated	15.00	14.00

PRICES OF COMBINATION COLONY BROODERS.

No. 1.—(Outdoor) Floor space 36x72 ins.—weight, crated, 300 lbs.	$20.00	$18.00
No. 2.—(Outdoor) Floor space 30x60 ins.—weight, crated 208 lbs.	16.00	14.40
No. 3.—(Outdoor) Floor space 27x48 ins.—weight, crated, 150 lbs.	12.00	10.80
Hover, with lamp case, smoke conductor, lamp and thermometer.	7.00	6.40
When used indoors alone, lamp case is not required.		
Hover and lamp, with smoke pipes	6.00	5.45
With regulator attached ... extra..	1.00	.90

This hover is what we use in all our popular Colony brooders. It can be used in any style of box, brooder or colony house.

SPECIAL: Dealers' Orders will be Freighted from Factory Prepaid.

Complete Prairie State Catalogue with half-tone illustrations showing all different style incubators and brooders, actual dimensions and shipping weights, mailed free upon application.

VAUGHAN'S "ZENITH" HEN FEED.

Vaughan's Zenith Hen Feed is different from nearly every hen food on the market. It contains no grit, no shell or other weight-making ingredients. Every ounce of "**Zenith Feed**" is an ounce of pure grain. The feed is composed of only sound, sweet grain, as we never, under any condition, allow any damaged grain to get into this food. The mixture is made carefully and scientifically. We believe this Feed to be the cleanest and best balanced ration on the market today. Because **Zenith** is an all-grain mixture, it is advisable in feeding to supply, in addition, Grit, Bone, Meat Meal, Charcoal and Green Food. If fed in a litter of cut clover or hay, scratching is necessary and is an extremely beneficial exercise for the poultry. Samples and prices mailed on application.

VAUGHAN'S A. AND C. CHICK FOOD.

This is a specially prepared, balanced ration food for young chicks which meets the full requirements for growth, health and perfect development. There are two grades, designed for best results at all ages of the chick.

Grade A.—For chicks up to four weeks old.

Grade C.—For chicks four weeks to four months old. **Samples and Prices on Application.**

Pigeon Food.—Put up in one grade only, as a whole food for young pigeons and a foundation food for large birds.

We put up A. and C. Chick Food and Pigeon Food in handsome 5-lb. lithographed cartons to retail at 25c per carton; one dozen packages, $2.50.

GRIT AND SHELLS.

	Per ton.	100 lbs.
Vaughan's **Complete Pearl Grit**, in 3 grades, Nos. 1, 2, 3.	$12.00	$0.65
Foust's Health Grit for Pigeons		1.75
Crushed Oyster Shells	13.00	.70

Cartage on Grit and Shells, 25c on less than 10 sacks.

GROUND BONE.

	100 LBS
Granulated for young chicks, 25 lbs., 60c; 50 lbs., $1.10	2.00
Coarse, for full grown fowl, 25 lbs., 60c; 50 lbs., $1.10	2.00

CHARCOAL.

This aids in digestion and sweetens the contents of the crop.

Chick and hen size, 25 lbs., 60c; 50 lbs., $1.00 .... 1.75

ALFALFA CLOVER MEAL.

The best substitute for green grass.

Vaughan's **Alfalfa Meal**, 50-lb. bags, $1.10 .... 2.00

POULTRY FOODS.

	Doz.
Conkey's **Laying Tonic**, 25c size, each, 20c	$2.25
Conkey's **Laying Tonic**, 50c size, each, 40c	4.50
Pratt's Poultry Food, 25c size, each, 20c	2.35
Pratt's Poultry Food, 60c size, each, 50c	5.40

Dried Blood Meal, 25, 50, or 100 lbs. Prices on application; subject to market changes.

Meat and Bone, 25, 50, or 100 lbs. Prices on application; subject to market changes.

Beef Scraps, 25, 50, or 100 lbs. Prices on application; subject to market changes.

EGG PRODUCERS.

		DOZ
Vaughan's "Zenith,"	15c size, each, 12c	1.25
" "	25c size, each, 20c	2.25
" "	50c size, each, 40c	4.70

BIRD SEED

We list the following: Canary, Hemp, Rape, Sunflower and Mixed. Prices on application, subject to market changes.

STOCK FOODS.

Pratt's, 50c size only, each, 40c	4.50
Conkey's Stock Vigor, 25c size, each, 20c	2.35
Conkey's Stock Vigor, 50c size, each, 40c	4.50

LICE POWDER.

Sandford's, 16-oz. size, ea., 20c; doz., $2.25. 40 oz. size, ea., 40c; doz. 4.25

100 oz. size, 85c each; doz 9.50

LICE POWDERS—Continued.

Conkey's 15 oz. size, each, 20c; doz..............$2.25
" 48.oz., size, each, 40c; doz............. 4.50
" 100 oz. size, each, 80c; doz............. 9.00

LIQUID LICE KILLERS.

Rice's 1 gal. size, each, 75c; doz............... 9.00
" 2 qt. size, each, 50c; doz................. 5.50
" 1 qt. size, each, 25c; doz................. 2.75

Conkey's 1 gal. size, each, 75c; doz............$8.30
" 2 qt. size, each, 50c; doz............ 5.75
" 1 qt. size, each, 30c; doz............ 3.50

Sulphur Candles, Vaughan's 10c size, each 8c; doz. 95c

PIGEON AND POULTRY REMEDIES.

Roup Cure, Vaughan's Good Health, Liquid, 50c size, each, 40c; doz. 4.25
" " " " " " 25c size, each, 20c; doz. 2.25
" " " Powder, 50c size, each, 40c; doz. 4.25
" " " " $1.00 size, each, 75c; doz. 8.00
" " Vaughan's Magic Liquid.............25c size, $2.25 per doz.
50c size, each, 40c............................per doz.. 4.25
Roup Cure, Conkey's, 50c size, each, 40c; doz., $4.00; $1.00 size, each, 75c; doz. 8.50
Vaughan's Good Health Tablets, per box, 40c; doz. boxes.......... 3.50

LEG BANDS FOR POULTRY.

Leader, doz., 10c; 50, 35c; 100............................... .60
Smith Sealed, doz., 20c; 50, 65c; 100........................... 1.25
Improved Champion, doz., 10c; 50, 35c; 100...................... .60

SANFORD'S "ZENITH" FLY KNOCKER.

An effective remedy against flies and mosquitoes; also lice, screw worms and horn and blow flies.
It kills lice on horses, cows and other animals.

Sandford's 1 gal. size, each.................$1.00
" 2 qt. size, each................. .65
" 1 qt. size, each................. .40

MILK OIL LIQUID DISINFECTANT

As a general disinfectant and cleaner stands without an equal. Infallible destroyer of all vermin and disease germs. Certain eradicator of insects and disease of all animals. Kills Cockroaches, Water Bugs, Ants, etc.

Pint size, each, 23c; doz............................$2.25
Quart size, each 35c; doz........................... 4.00
Half gal. size, each, 65c; doz...................... 6.50

We carry several other Lice Killing Powders and Liquids, Disinfectants and Poultry Remedies. We are headquarters for Bird Seeds of all kinds.

DRINKING FOUNTAINS

		EACH.	DOZ.
Vaughan's Galvanized Iron, 2	qts.	$0.45	$ 4.65
" " " 4	"	.60	7.00
" " " 8	"	.90	10.00
Stoneware 1	"	.18	2.00
" 2	"	.25	2.75
" 4	"	.30	3.25
Peerless 5	"	.45	4.75
" 10	"	.75	9.80
Prairie State 1	"	.20	2.00
" " 2	"	.25	2.50
" " 4	"	.30	3.25
" " 8	"	.45	4.75
Moe's Top-Fill Fountain 1	gal.	1.10	
" " " 2	"	1.55	
" " " 4	"	1.95	
Vaughan's Galvanized Brooder Fountain 2	qts.	.50	5.50

VAUGHAN'S FOUNTAIN.

SHIPPING COOPS.

All-Wood Shipping Coops. No. 1, each, 30c; doz., $3.00. No. 2, each, 35c; doz., $3.50. No. 3, each, 35c; doz., $3.50. No. 4 each, 40c; doz., $4.25. No. 5, each, 50c; doz., $5.25. No. 6 each, 55c; doz., $5.75.

Vaughan's Exhibition Coop. Trio size, each, $1.90; pen size, each....$2.00

MISCELLANEOUS.

Petty Poultry Punch, each, 18c; doz.......$2.00
Spring Lever Punch, each, 18c; per doz..... 2.00
Poultry Killing Knife (Pilling), each, 40c; doz.4.50
Egg Carriers, Reliable. 12 doz., ea., 40c; doz.4.50
" " Reliable. 15 doz., ea., 50c.; doz.5.50
" " Gem. 15 per cent off retail list.
Egg Boxes, Eyrie, 1 setting, doz., $1.20; 5 doz. 5.75
Egg Boxes, Eyrie, 2 setting, doz., $1.65; 5 doz. 8.00

SPRING LEVER.

Grit Boxes, (Vaughan's wooden), each, 35c; per doz......$3.40
" " **Sanitary,** (Galvanized), each, 45c; per doz.. 6.00

Dry Food Hopper. This is a strong, galvanized iron box, similar to the grit and shell box, except that it is larger and has but two compartments, one twice the size of the other. The larger one is intended for grain, the smaller for beef scraps. Each...........$0.70
Per dozen 7.75

Nest Eggs, porcelain, doz., 20c; gross 2.00
" " Reynold's Medicated, doz., 50c; per gross.......... 5.50
Pigeon Nests, (Earthenware), per doz., $1.10; per 100.......... 8.00
" " (Wooden), per doz., 90c; per 100.......... 7.50
" Perches, Muir's Iron, per doz., 85c; per 100.......... 6.50
" " Jersey, per doz., 60c; per 100.......... 4.75
Caponizing Sets, complete, with book of instructions.......... 2.00

American Feed Trough. The best feed trough ever put on the market. Made in three sizes. No. 1, 18 ins. long, each, 50c; doz., $5.50. No. 2, 24 ins. long, each, 75c; doz., $8.00. No. 3, 30 ins. long, each, $1.00; doz. $11.00

Wire Hens' Nests, each, 13c; doz.......... 1.40

Poultry Netting. Prices on application.

Salt Cat for Pigeons. Salt Cat is a scientific combination of those aromatic and tonic properties contained in such seeds and roots as gentian, anise, coriander, etc., combined with sulphur, charcoal, limestone, salt, bone and other materials that are generally recognized by pigeon keepers as aiding digestion, promoting good health and egg production in pigeons and game fowls. Price, per doz. bricks,........$1.50

VAUGHAN'S PARKS LAWN SEED

2 lb. box.

5 lb. box.

1 lb. box.

VAUGHAN'S LAWN GRASS SEED.

Vaughan's Lawn Grass Seed has been known as a quality mixture for thirty-five years. A dealer can sell it with the assurance that there is no better grade put up and a customer will accept it without argument.

Grass Seed, after several high priced years, is down again to normal prices. With great care we select the fanciest samples of the different grasses the market offers, and our mixtures are properly balanced, the result of thirty-six years' experience, and are made of the fanciest samples of the different grasses. An equal quality mixture cannot be sold for less money.

VAUGHAN'S "CHICAGO PARKS" Highest Grade

Package Quantity Prices.
Half pound (sell for 15c each), per 100 .... $ 8.50
One pound (sell for 25c each) per 100 .... 16.00
Five pounds (sell for $1.00 each), per 100 lbs 15.00
Bulk, per 100 lbs 14.00

OUR OTHER STANDARD MIXTURES.

COLUMBIAN "SHADY NOOK" LAWN GRASS MIXTURE, for shaded places, under trees, etc. Price same as Chicago Parks.

"QUICK SHOW" LAWN SEED, for immediate effect. 10 lbs $1.40; 100 lbs. 12.00

"GOOD MIXED" LAWN GRASS SEED. 10 lbs., $1.35, 100 lbs.... 10.00

			100 lbs.	
KENTUCKY BLUE GRASS. Fancy Clean (21 lb. seed)	14 lbs.,	$1.50	$12.00	Subject to change without notice.
RED TOP, Fancy Seed. Extra heavy	10 lbs.,	1.50	12.00	
" " Unhulled	10 lbs.,	0.70	6.00	

CLOVER, DUTCH WHITE. Very fine quality. Write for prices.

Terms on all Grasses or Clovers strictly cash.

VAUGHAN'S LAWN FERTILIZER

THE BEST LAWN DRESSING ON THE MARKET—

Odorless, Lasting and Effective
A Good Seller.

Prices:

	100 lbs.	1000 lbs.
In 5 and 10-lb. pkgs...	$2.90	$28.50
In 25 and 50-lb. bags..	2.45	21.50
In 100-lb. bags	2.25	18.50

WE TAKE PLEASURE IN CALLING ATTENTION TO VAUGHAN'S SPECIALTIES FOR 1912

Below we mention some of the most important vegetable seed and gladioli novelties and specialties which we are able to offer in a wholesale way.

GLADIOLI.

KUNDERDI GLORY. The broadly expanded, wide open flowers, paired by twos, all face in the same direction and are carried on straight stout stalks, fully 3½ feet. From three to eight of these handsome flowers are open at one time. Each petal is exquisitely ruffled and fluted. Color delicate cream pink, with a most attractive crimson stripe in the center of each lower petal, the shade of which is unique in Gladioli.

Price, per 100, $5.00; per 1,000 .... $43.00

MRS. FRANCIS KING. The long, strong flower stalks with foliage, and its effective flower spike with a good line of reserve buds continually opening, and with flowers 4½ inches across, and five to six flowers well spread out on the spike at the same time, gives for vases, in hotel lobbies and dining rooms, parlor decorations, etc., an effect not produced by any other Gladiolus. The color is brilliant Flamingo pink blazed with vermilion red.

First size, per 100, $2.25; per 1,000 .... $20.00

CHICAGO WHITE—Novelty of 1912. Flowers are well expanded, well placed upon the stalk, pure white with faint lavender streaks in the lower petals. In form they resemble the Childsii type. They are borne on tall, straight stems and from 5 to 7 flowers are open at one time. It is one of the earliest varieties to bloom.

Price, per 100 .... $7.50

VEGETABLE SEEDS.

BEANS—We raise on our own farm in Central Michigan and under our direct supervision, the very fanciest grades of Bush Garden Beans, both Wax and Green Pod. For such stocks we charge no more than jobbers who have carelessly grown, uninspected and unrogued seed.

We call particular attention to the following:

Stringless Green Pod, Longfellow, Red Valentine, Black Valentine, Improved Golden Wax, Davis Wax, Wardwell's Wax.

Write for prices in quantity for contract next season.

SWEET CORN—Malakoff, the finest quality extra early variety. Per bushel, $4.50.

GOLDEN BANTAM—A fine crop of our own raising.

10-bushel lots at $3.50.

CUCUMBER—Davis Perfect, a fancy strain, our own growing. Hence the introduction of the variety.

Per lb., 65c; 10 lbs., $6.50.

LETTUCE—All seasons. Our introducer's strain is the best by far.

Lb., 55c; 100 lbs., $50.00.

MUSKMELONS AND WATERMELONS—We have special strains grown under our direct control—many absolutely unequaled in the trade.

MUSKMELONS—Vaughan's Original Osage, Paul Rose, Hoodoo, Extra Early Hackensack, and Emerald Gem.

WATERMELONS — Cole's Early, Kleckley Sweet, Black Diamond, and Sweetheart.

PEAS—Laxtonian, the most startling novelty of recent years, a dwarf Gradus.

Per bushel, $8.00.

TOMATO—Fancy Jersey Strains, of **popular novelties, at the right** prices.

Earliana, Bonny Best, **Hummer, Early Detroit, Livingston's Globe,** Coreless, etc.

Lightning Source UK Ltd.
Milton Keynes UK
UKHW020622060119
334855UK00006B/462/P